רוקט

צירית שום

ארוגולה

SHELLY'S
HUMBLE
KITCHEN

25 Salad Ballads
Copyright © 2025 by Shelly Gilad
Food photographs copyright © 2025 by Shelly Gilad
Illustrations copyright © 2025 by Shelly Gilad

All rights reserved. No part of this book may be reproduced, distributed, or transmitted in any form or by any means, including photocopying, recording, or other electronic or mechanical methods, without the prior written permission of the author, except in the case of brief quotations embodied in critical reviews and certain other noncommercial uses permitted by copyright law.

Cover and book design by Studio Greenfield
Photographs and Illustrations by Shelly Gilad

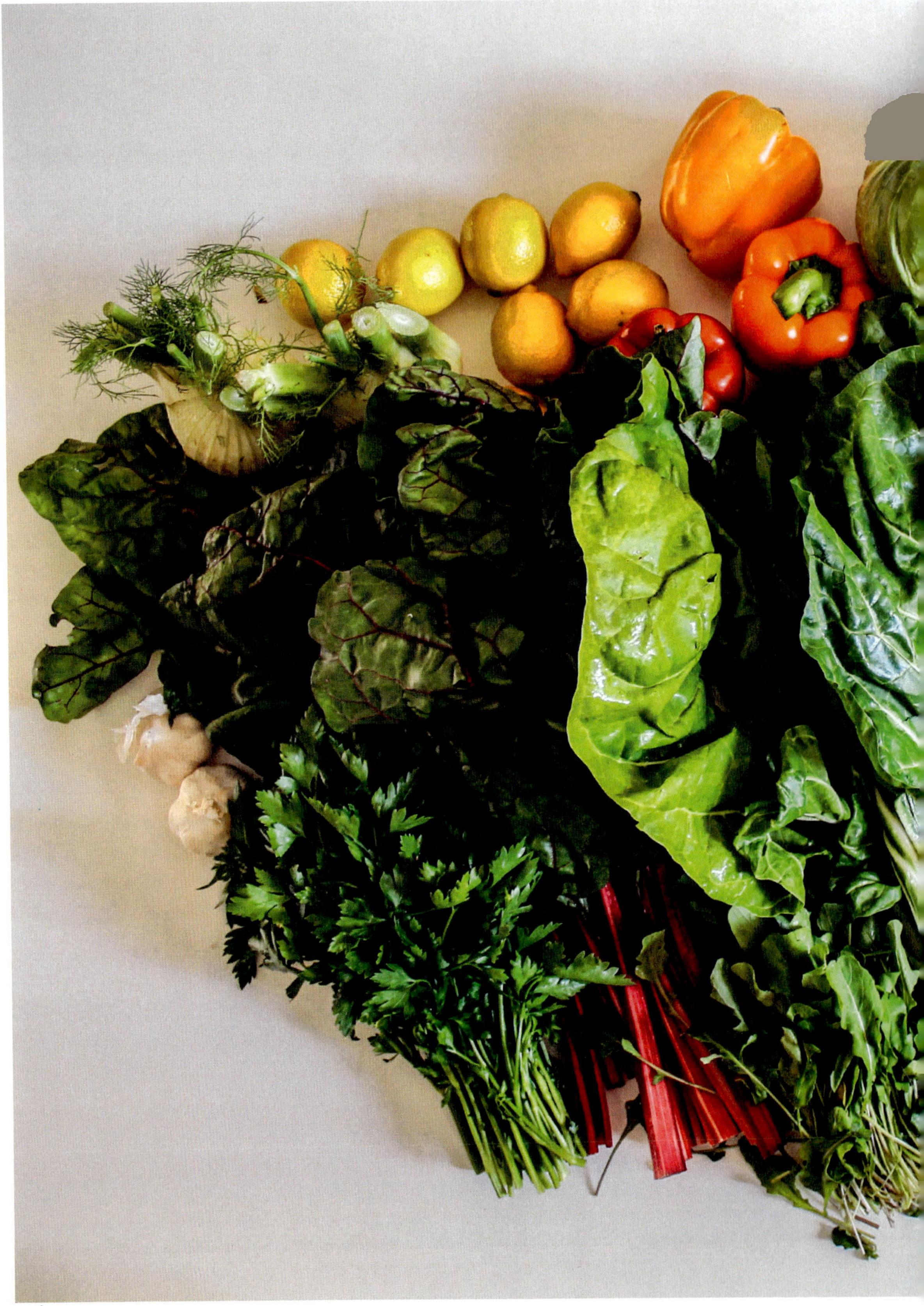

Eama and Aba,

Thank you for making such a big fuss about vegetables and herbs.

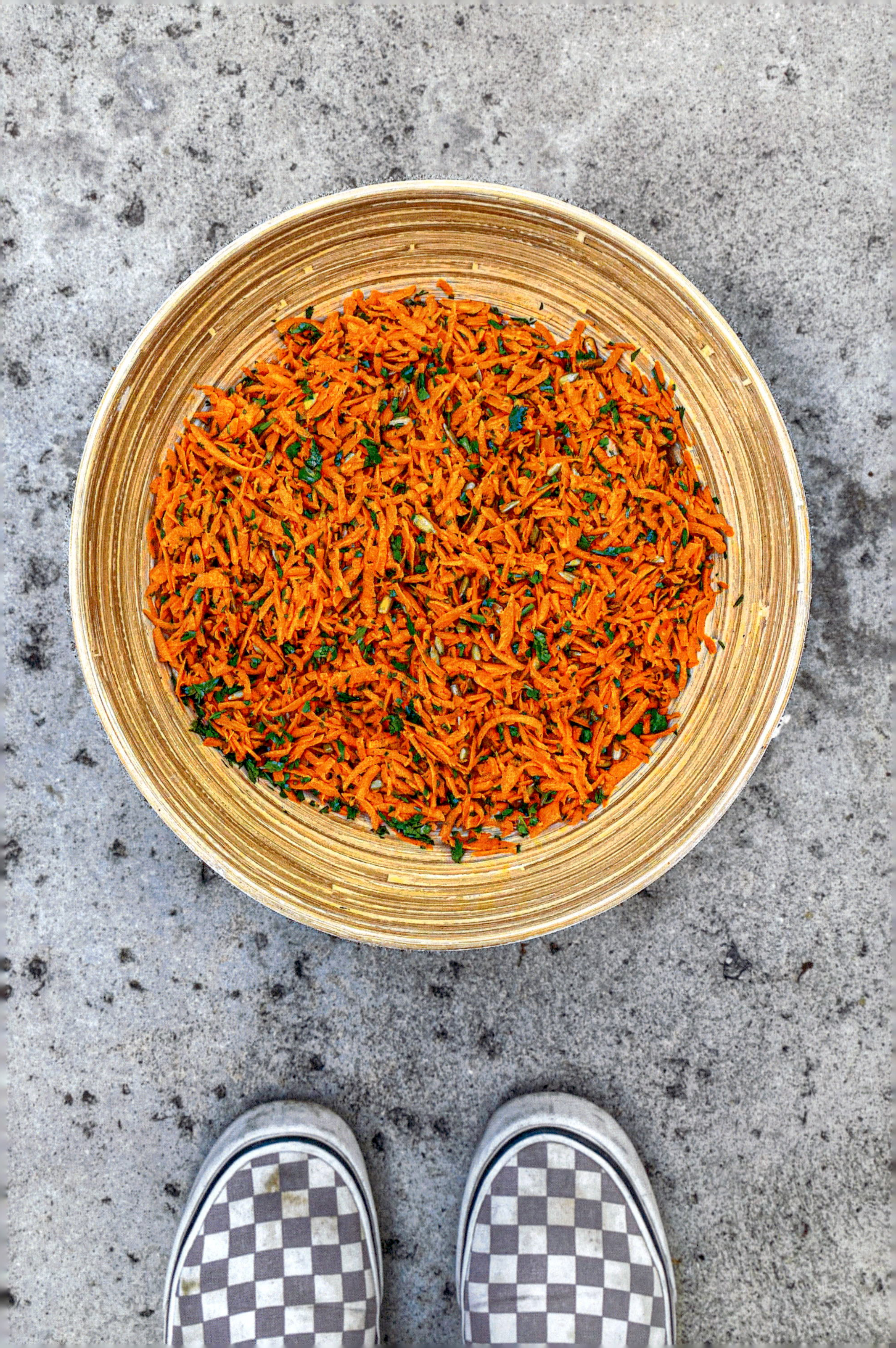

SALAD BALLADS

25 Unique & Easy Everyday Salads

SHELLY GILAD

CONTENTS

HELLO! IS IT ME YOU WERE LOOKING FOR?   12

    Determining the Salad Portion   14

    Dressing Your salad   14

    Tips for Washing & Storing Vegetables   15

    The Little Book of Great Salads Playlist   15

    Basic Pantry   19

CHAPTER ONE: EVERYDAY I'M SHUFFLING   21

    Breakfast Chopped Salad   23

    Cucumber, Scallion, peanuts & Chili Oil   25

    Eema's Spicy Tomato Salad   27

    5-4-3-2-1 Corn Salsa   29

    Greek-ish Salad   31

CHAPTER TWO: JIFFY LEAFY   33

    How to tell if your greens are fresh   34

    Salat Estee   37

    Lettuce, Corn, Cucumber & Snap Peas   39

    Arugula Cucumber Salad with Za'atar Croutons   41

    Wedding Herb Salad   45

CHAPTER THREE: TUTTI-FRUTTI   46

    Asian Pear, Celery, Snap Peas & Toasted Almonds   49

    Phenomenal Fennel, Arugula & persimmon Salad   51

    Bloody Waldorf Salad   52

    Lettuce, Zucchini & Nectarine salad   55

    Winter Fruit Salad   57

CHAPTER FOUR: THE SCENIC ROOTS   58

    Our Everyday Root Salad   61

    Aba's Quick-Pickled Roots   63

    May The Best Carrot Salad Win   65

CHAPTER FIVE: COOKED SALADS   66

    5-Minute Broccoli Salad   69

    North-African Carrot Salad   71

    Quinoa Salad with Herbs, Pomelo and Almonds 72

    Elvis Parsley Potato Salad   75

    Celery Salad Over Celeriac Hummus   77

    Wild Thing, You Make My Rice Sing!   81

    Smoky Cauliflower Salad with Tahini   85

    Awfully Good Chickpea Salad   86

ABOUT THE AUTHOR   88

Tomatoes, onion, parsley, olive oil, salt & pepper

A4
家庭保障，免稅退休規劃
Cynthia Lau, CPA
Agency Director, Tax Advisor
909-569-3535
Celina Sun
Diane Liou
Maurice Yang
Agency Director
David Chia
Agency Director
Tung
626-945-0188
SCAN ME
美國泛宇集團
兩個策

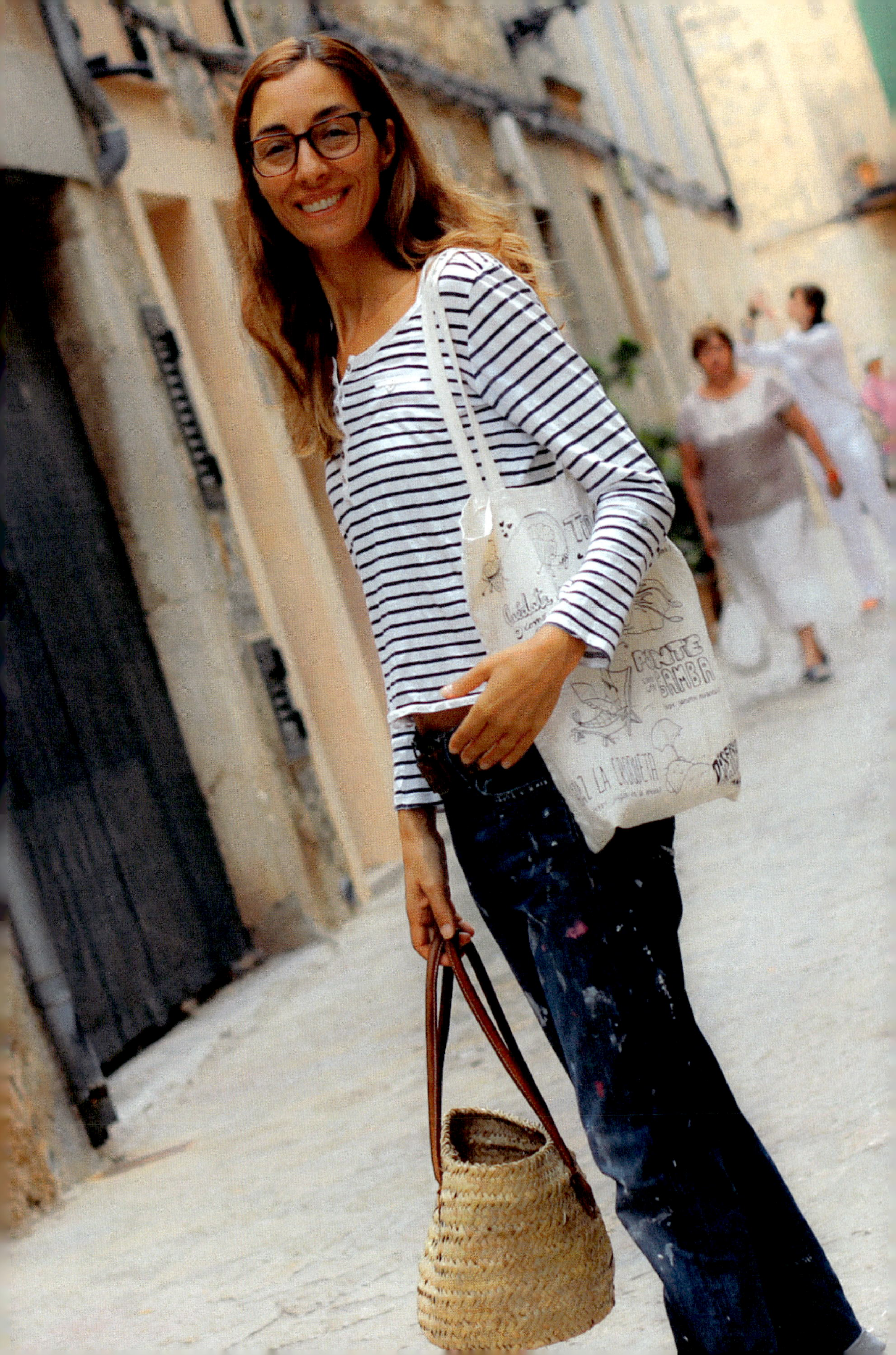

HELLO! IS IT ME YOU WERE LOOKING FOR?

While I'm still waiting for my first cookbook proposal to find a publishing home, I decided not to waste any time and I started working on what was supposed to be my second book, but with a twist: instead of trying to publish the entire thing at once, which is extremely overwhelming when you have to do everything yourself – the cooking, styling, photographing, writing, writing in a second language, illustrating – I had the idea to publish it online, chapter by chapter.

I chose to lead off with the salad chapter. Stats from my blog and social media indicated that I'm not the only one eating salads daily with breakfast, lunch and dinner. Not necessarily for health reasons, but because this is how I was raised.

Growing up in a Moroccan-Israeli home, we always had a fresh chopped salad on the table with every meal. My mother or father wouldn't sit down until that salad was on the table, whether it was cucumber scallion (page 25), spicy tomato (page 27) quick pickled roots (page 65). But they never made the dressing separately; they put the olive oil, lemon juice, salt and pepper straight into the salad bowl, and tossed it with their hands. I do the same, unless I'm making a dressing that needs emulsifying first and in advance.

Most days I make simple two-ingredient salads like my 5-Minute Broccoli Salad (page 71). Other times I make more effort and prepare more elaborate salads like, my Wild Rice Salad (page 83). We rarely have salad leftovers in our house – my boys fight over the salad and even over the salad juice at the bottom of the bowl.

Friends who come over for meals are usually surprised by the fact that we rarely drink water while dining. Even as kids, we didn't have that glass of water tradition. I realize now it was unnecessary because our meals always contained lots of hydrating vegetables.

Thank you for buying my book and trusting my taste buds. May these salads energize you and color your days, like they do for us.

DETERMINING THE SALAD PORTION

The amount of salad you make depends on how many people are eating and what other dishes will accompany it. You determine the quantity based on a rough guideline of how many vegetables per person. For example, for my May the Best Carrot Salad Win (page 67) I use four medium shredded carrots per person. For a side romaine salad that will accompany roasted chicken meant to serve four people, I would use an entire head of romaine lettuce. However, if the salad is intended as the main meal, you'll want to add some protein like chicken, eggs, beans, etc., to make it more filling and nutritious.

DRESSING YOUR SALAD

My mother couldn't stand the smell of vinegar so I didn't like it until I was in highschool. Over the years I developed a taste for it. Now I use it often but not instead of lemon juice. Most of my salads call for lemon juice, which I am hoping wouldn't be an obstacle for those of you living in Antarctica or other lemon-scarce climes. You want to hit that sweet spot where it's slightly acidic, slightly sweet, and slightly salty.

My go-to everyday dressing is a simple mix of olive oil, lemon juice, apple cider vinegar, salt, black pepper, and sometimes a touch of honey or maple syrup. If I put fruit in the salad, I skip the sweetener altogether.

Now, if you're new to the kitchen or you've never made a salad before, listen up. This is a crucial tip: always, and I mean always, add the dressing right before you're ready to serve. If you dress your mixed green salad too early, it will get soggy by the time you sit down to eat. It's better to wait until the very last minute to toss that salad with the dressing, right before you bring it to the table.

TIPS FOR WASHING & STORING VEGETABLES

- ❖ Proper washing and storage of vegetables is crucial for maintaining freshness, flavor, and nutritional value. Here are some tips to help you get the most out of your produce:

- ❖ Wash vegetables just before using them, not before storing. Excess moisture can lead to faster spoilage. For example, vegetables like carrots and potatoes: Scrub gently under running water with a vegetable brush.

- Vegetables like broccoli or cauliflower: Soak in cold, salted water for a few minutes to draw out any insects. Rinse thoroughly under running water.

- To wash leafy greens: Fill a salad spinner1 or large bowl with cold water. Submerge the greens and swish them around gently. Let them sit for a few minutes to allow dirt to settle. Lift the greens out, drain the water and spin to dry. Repeat until the leaves are pretty dry. (Take away my cutting board, but if you take away my salad spinner, I'll be devastated.)

- Refrigerate most vegetables in the crisper drawer.

- Store herbs like parsley and cilantro upright in a glass of water, covered loosely with a plastic bag.

- Keep onions, garlic, and potatoes in a cool, dark, dry place – not in the refrigerator.

- Store tomatoes at room temperature, away from direct sunlight.

- Keep mushrooms in a paper bag in the fridge.

- Store cut vegetables in airtight containers in the fridge.

- Keep ethylene-producing fruits (like apples and bananas) away from ethylene-sensitive vegetables to prevent premature ripening.

25 SALAD BALADS PLAYLIST

Music makes the people come together... just like food does. It makes cooking so much more fun, whether it's blasting at full volume or playing softly in the background. I like to play tunes that set me in the right mood for whatever I'm preparing. For instance, when cooking Indian cuisine, I'll play Bollywood tracks. If I'm cooking Moroccan food, then I play North African or Middle Eastern music. But with salads, it's usually an eclectic mix from around the world.

I've curated a playlist with some of my favorite songs for you to enjoy while preparing my salads. These tracks will get you in the mood and make the cooking feels less of a chore. You can find the "25 Salad Ballads" playlist on Spotify.

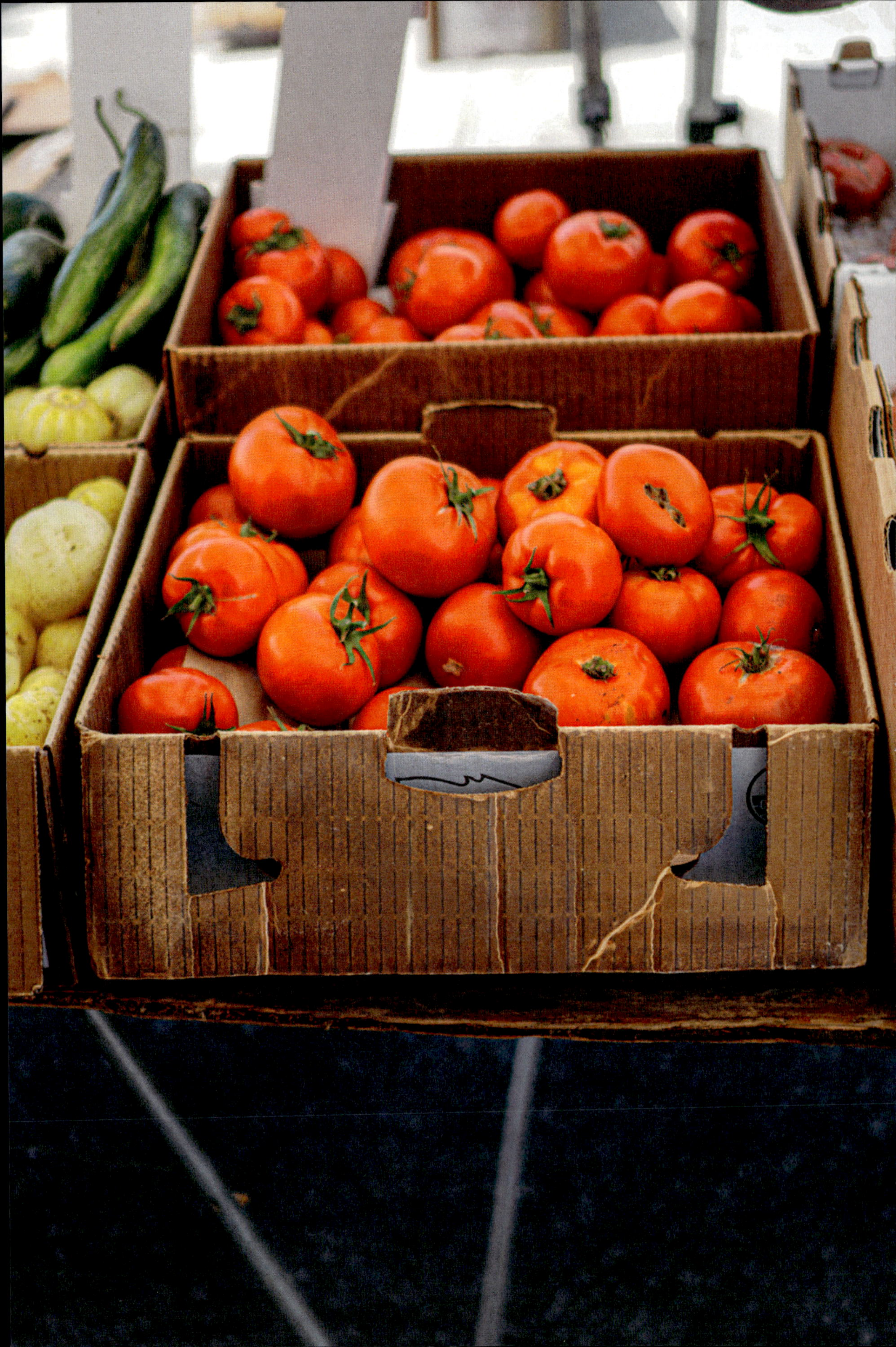

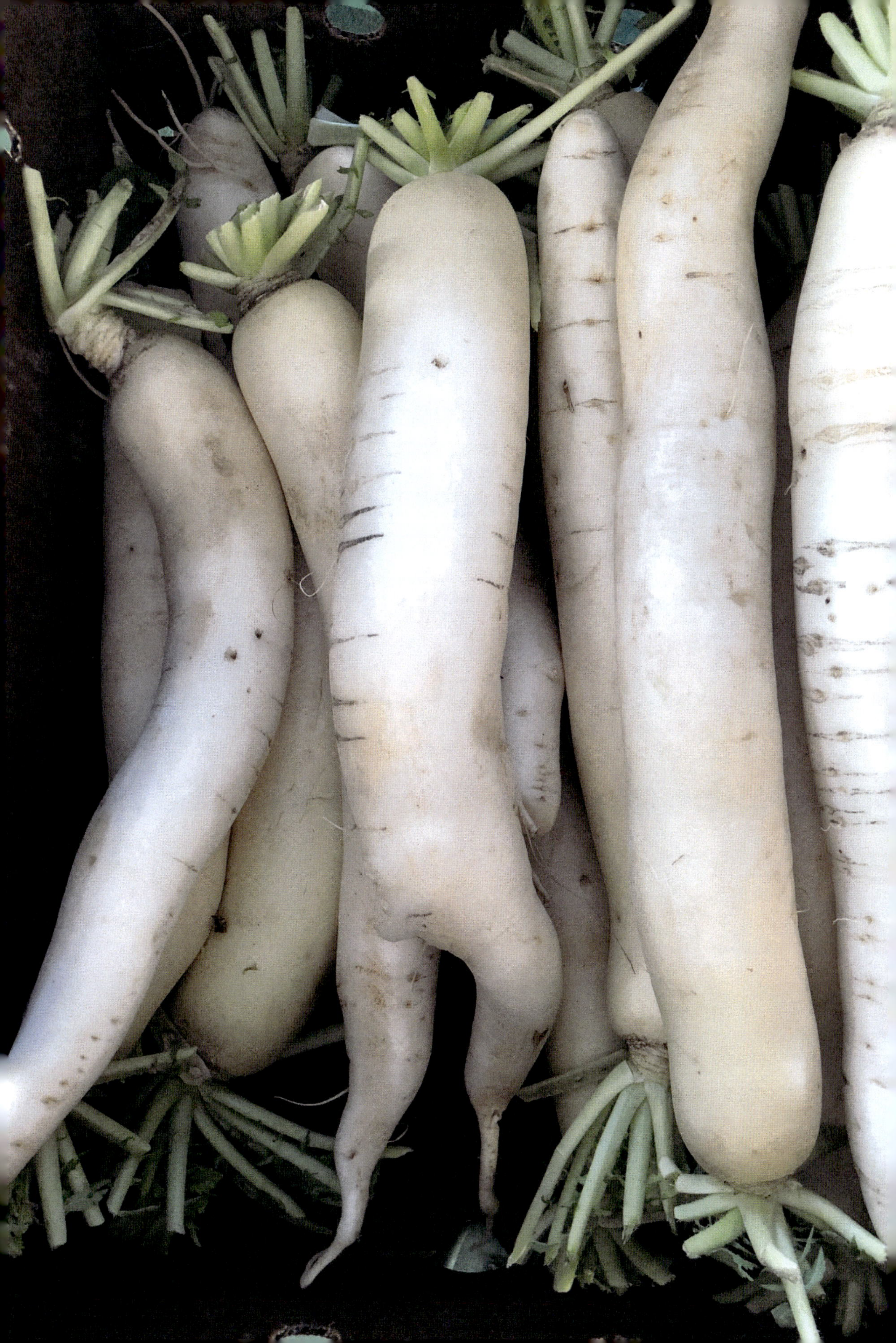

Lettuce	Kale	Spinach	Cucumber

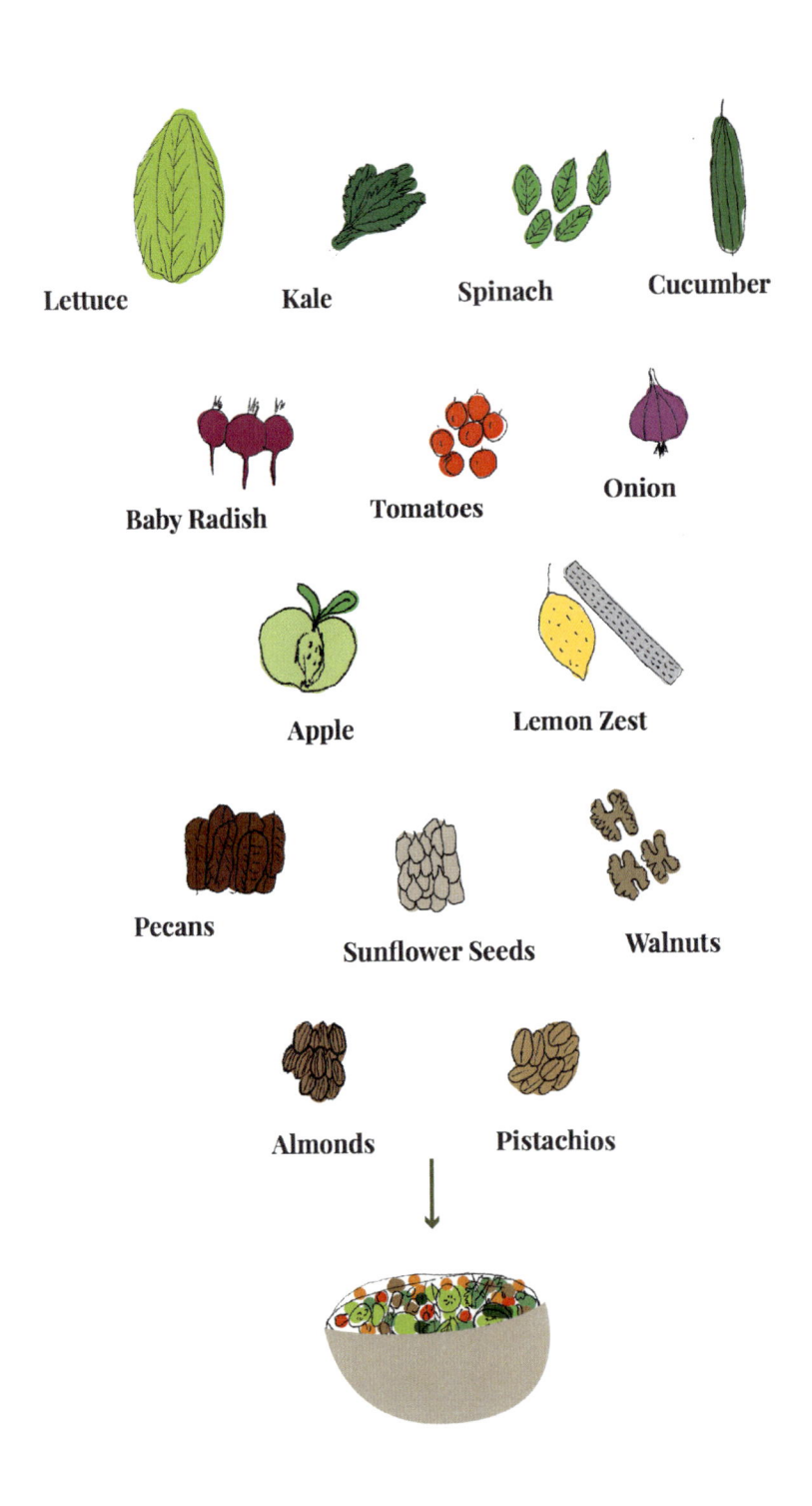

Baby Radish	Tomatoes	Onion

Apple	Lemon Zest

Pecans	Sunflower Seeds	Walnuts

Almonds	Pistachios

BASIC PANTRY

OILS AND VINEGARS

Olive oil

Avocado oil

Apple cider vinegar

Balsamic vinegar

Rice vinegar

SPICES AND HERBS

White pepper

Za'atar

Sumac

Cumin

Curry powder

Paprika

Salt and Pepper
While good sea salt and freshly ground pepper are preferred, basic salt and pre-ground pepper can still produce delicious dishes.

NUTS AND SEEDS

Almonds

Walnuts

Hazelnuts

Sunflower seeds

Pumpkin seeds

LEGUMES AND VEGETABLES

Canned or cooked legumes

Dry chickpeas

Canned corn

Preserved lemons or pickled limes

Barberries

CONDIMENTS AND SAUCES

Tahini
Preferably stone-ground, which is more runny and flavorful.

Harissa

Dijon mustard

Mayonnaise or vegan mayonnaise

Light soy sauce

Honey or maple syrup

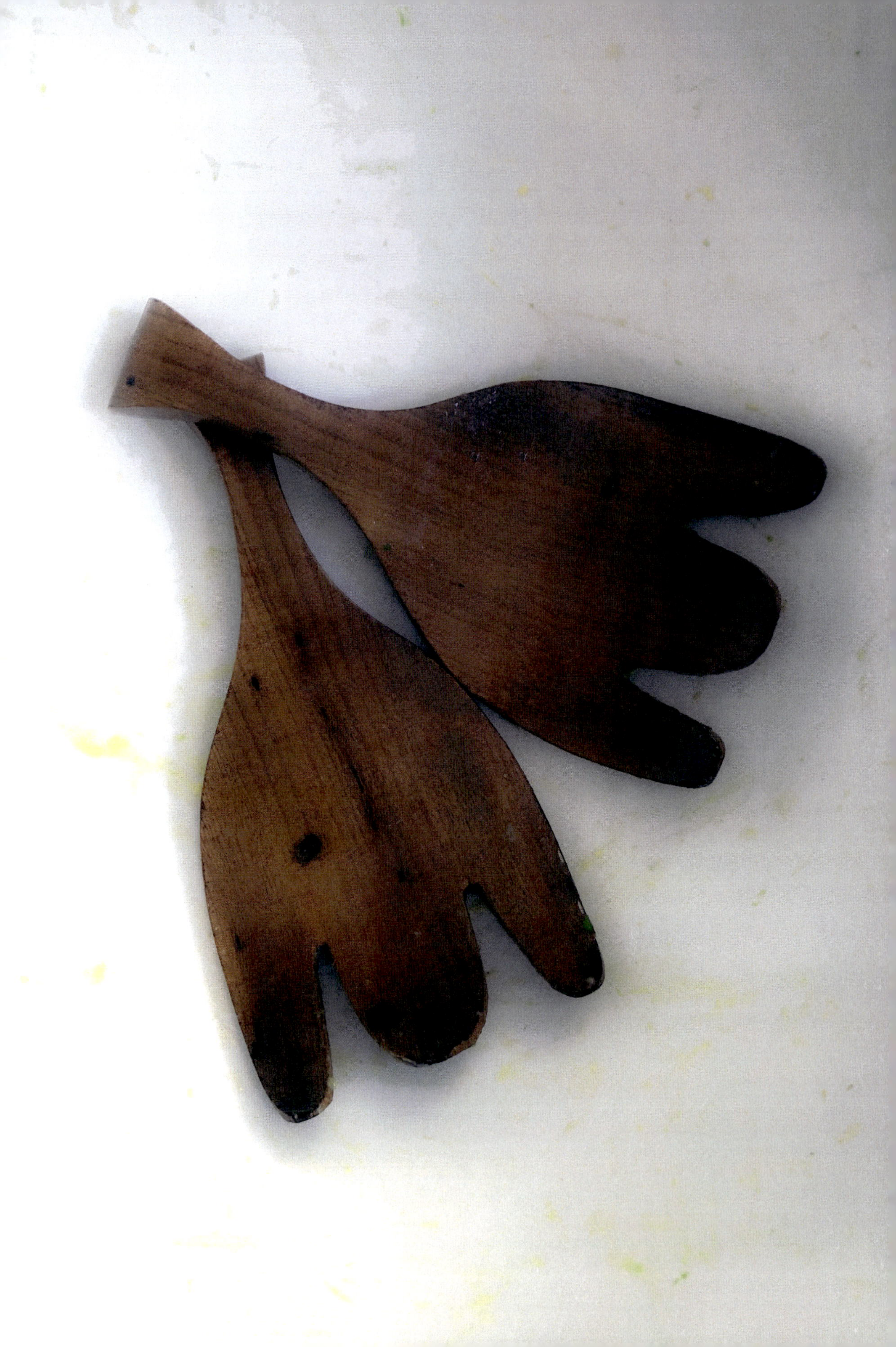

CHAPTER ONE

EVERYDAY I'M SHUFFLING

The magic of salads lies in their versatility – you can prepare a salad with just a lonely cucumber or go wild and toss in everything but the kitchen sink. The key is to consider the context of your meal. For example, if you've prepared a comforting bowl of soup for lunch, then a small grain salad with a low-water-content vegetable would be an ideal companion. On the other hand, if you're indulging in a rich, hearty stew or a plate of pasta, a light and refreshing leafy green salad with high water content would cut through the richness and cleanse your palate. By mastering the art of salad-making, you'll not only make your meals more exciting and nourishing but also experience food in a whole new way.

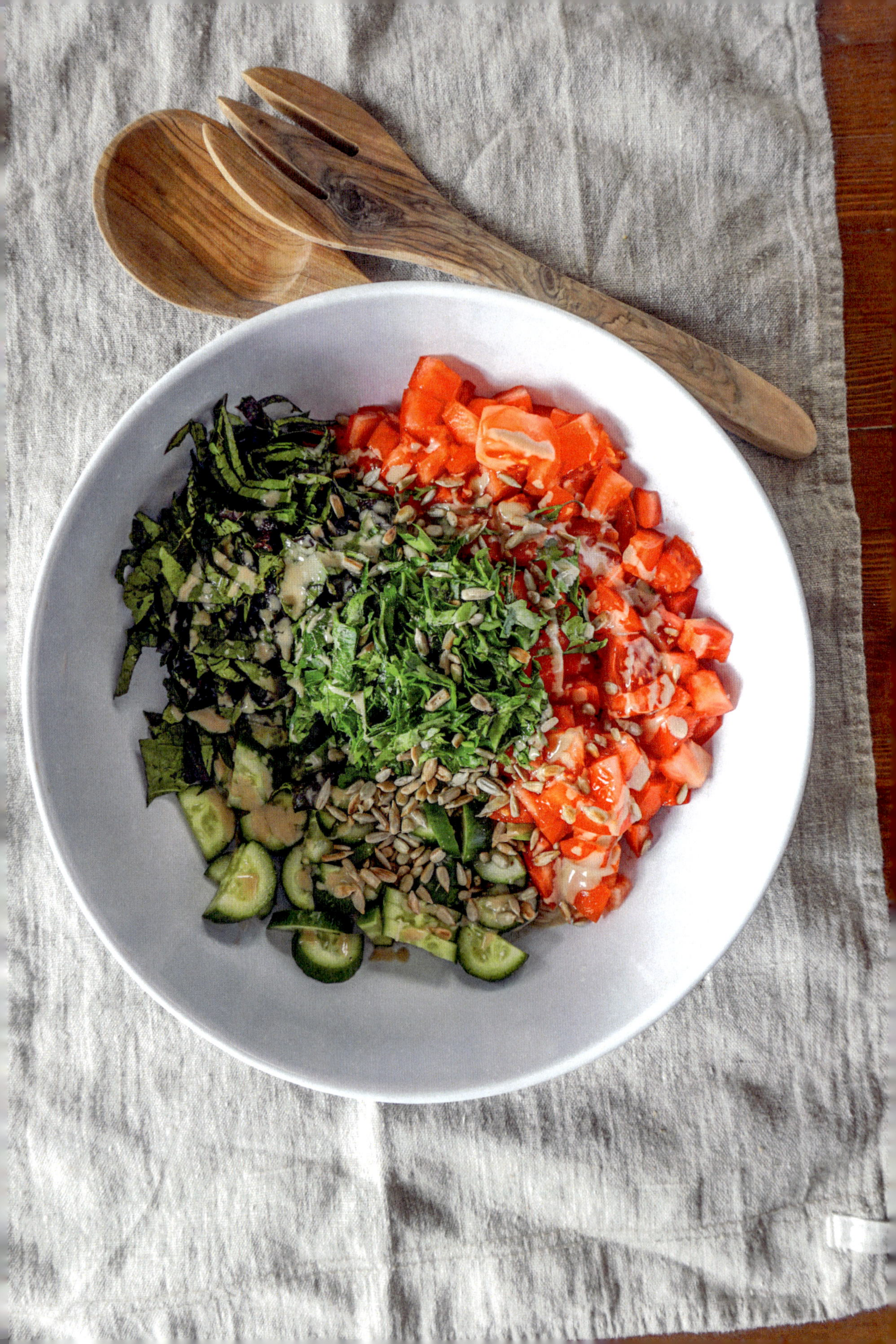

BREAKFAST CHOPPED SALAD

6 Romaine leaves (or another type of lettuce), chopped

4 medium tomatoes, diced

4 Persian cucumbers, sliced or diced

¼ cup parsley or cilantro, finely chopped

¼ cup toasted sunflower seeds

3 tablespoons fresh lemon juice

2 tablespoons tahini

2 tablespoons olive oil

Salt

Pepper

This is the kind of salad we have for breakfast in Israel. When you order a typical Israeli breakfast, you'll almost always get a version of this salad on the side. It's usually made with diced onions, but I skip those because the lingering aftertaste makes me crave something sweet afterward. I don't mind onion breath.

In the summer I like to add a sprig or two of mint leaves to make it more refreshing and cooling.

MAKES 2 TO 4 SERVINGS

In a large bowl, combine the chopped lettuce, diced tomatoes, cucumbers, and herbs. Add the sunflower seeds, lemon juice, tahini, and olive oil. Season with salt and pepper and toss well.

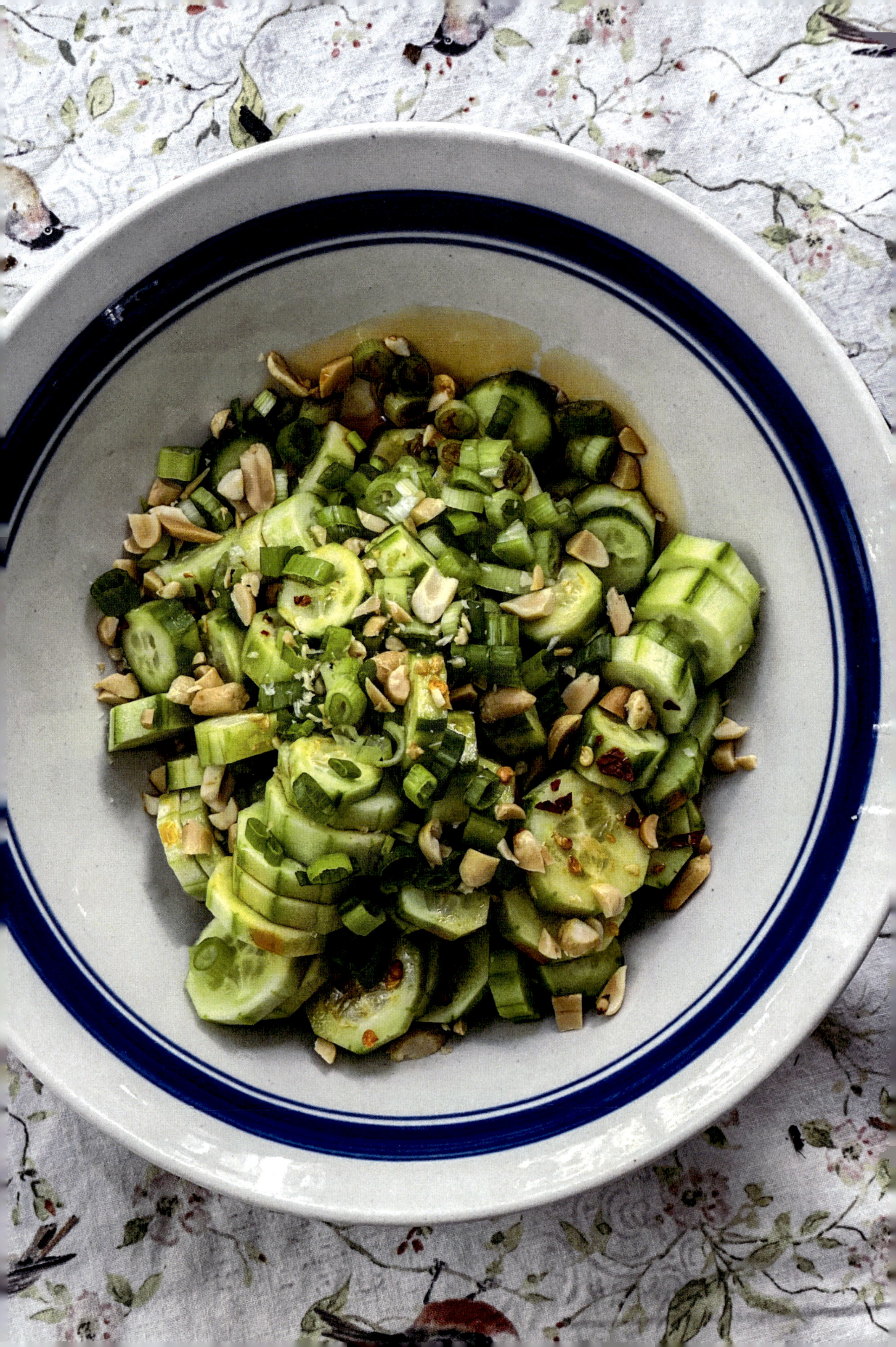

CUCUMBER, SCALLION, PEANUTS & CHILI OIL

8 Persian cucumbers, peeled and sliced

3 scallions, sliced

¼ cup toasted peanuts, crushed

2 tablespoons chili oil

1 tablespoon soy sauce

1 tablespoon rice vinegar

Whenever I have no energy to wash and dry leaves or chop lots of vegetables, I make this crunchy and delicious salad. With or without the peanuts. If you have the energy and time to chop a handful cilantro, go for it. It would make it even more Taiwanese.

MAKES 2 TO 4 SERVINGS

Combine all the ingredients in a medium bowl and toss well.

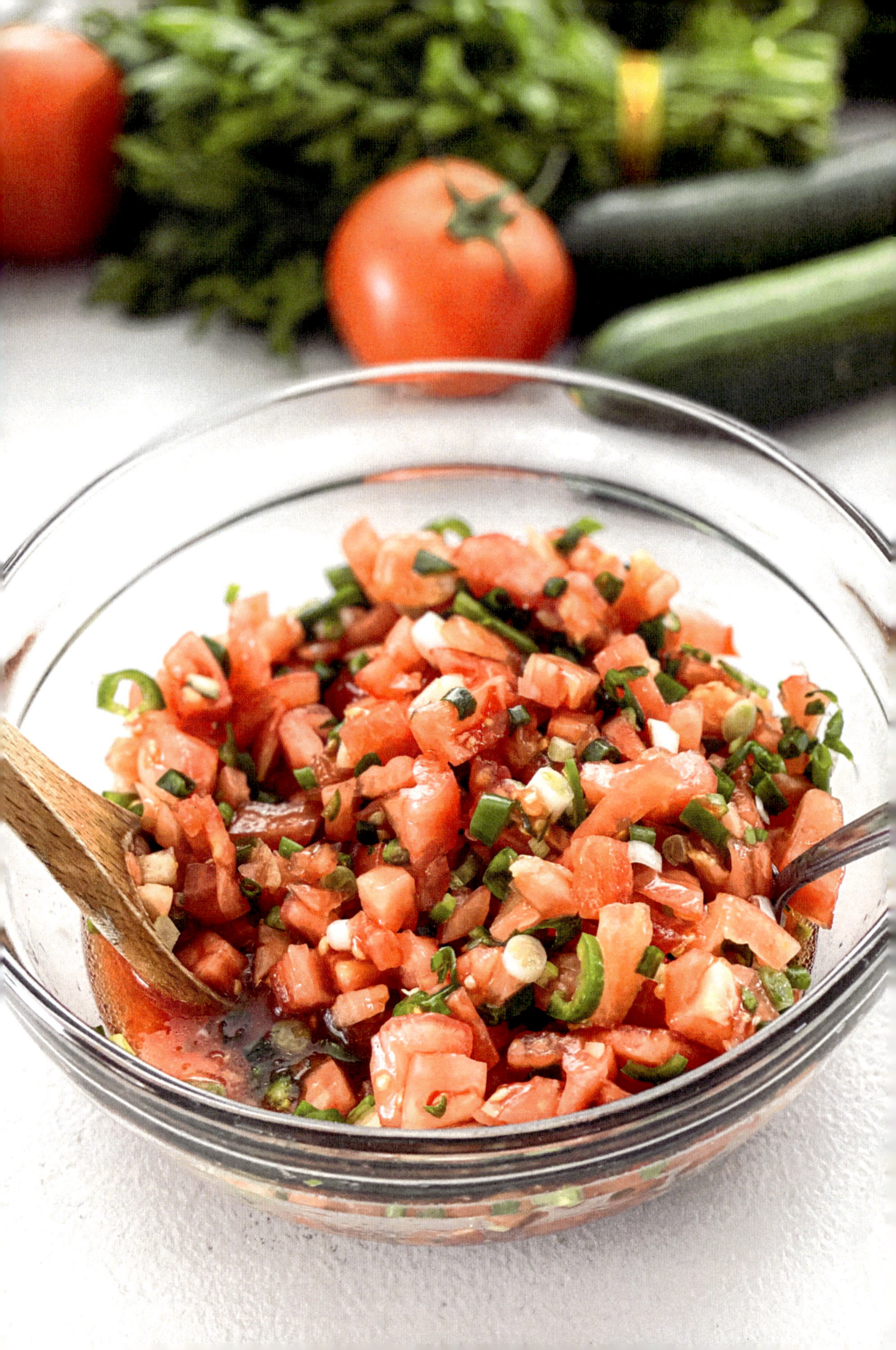

EEMA'S SPICY TOMATO SALAD

6 large tomatoes, peeled and diced

2 green chili peppers or jalapeños, seeded, deveined and sliced

3 scallions, sliced

3 tablespoons olive oil

3 tablespoons fresh lemon juice

Salt

Pepper

"Eema" means mother in Hebrew. This is the salad that my mom makes on a daily basis to accompany whatever she makes for lunch. It's a classic Middle Eastern salad, but hers is the best because she always peels the tomatoes, even when she's exhausted or in a rush. It makes a huge difference in the texture, not so much in the flavor, but still, I would peel the rubbery skin off tomatoes. It takes 5 more minutes, but it's worth it. It's pretty easy with a sharp vegetable peeler or a steak knife.

NOTES:

❖ The salad is supposed to be spicy, so if you're more of a mild-spicy kind of person, just swap in a milder green chili pepper.

❖ Best served fresh, but can be refrigerated for up to 1 day.

MAKES 2 TO 4 SERVINGS

Combine the diced tomatoes, chili peppers and scallions in a medium bowl. Add olive oil and lemon juice. Season with salt and pepper, toss well and serve immediately.

Salad Ballads

5-4-3-2-1 CORN SALSA

2 cups cooked corn kernels (about 4 corn ears)

¼ cup chopped cilantro

1 small red or white onion, chopped finely

1 jalapeño pepper, seeded, deveined and finely chopped

2 tablespoon fresh lime or lemon juice

Pinch ground cumin

Salt

Pepper

This salad is so basic, yet it is ridiculously delicious. I make it when corn is in season and costs about fifty cents per ear, and serve it with almost anything.

I've never made it with canned corn, but I'm sure it would be pretty good. If you can handle spice, leave some of the jalapeño seeds when you devein it.

MAKES 4 SERVINGS

Combine the corn, cilantro, onion and jalapeño in a medium bowl. Add the lime juice, season with cumin, salt and pepper and toss well. Serve immediately or store in the fridge for up to 2 days.

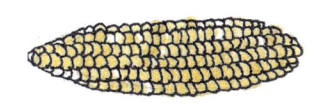

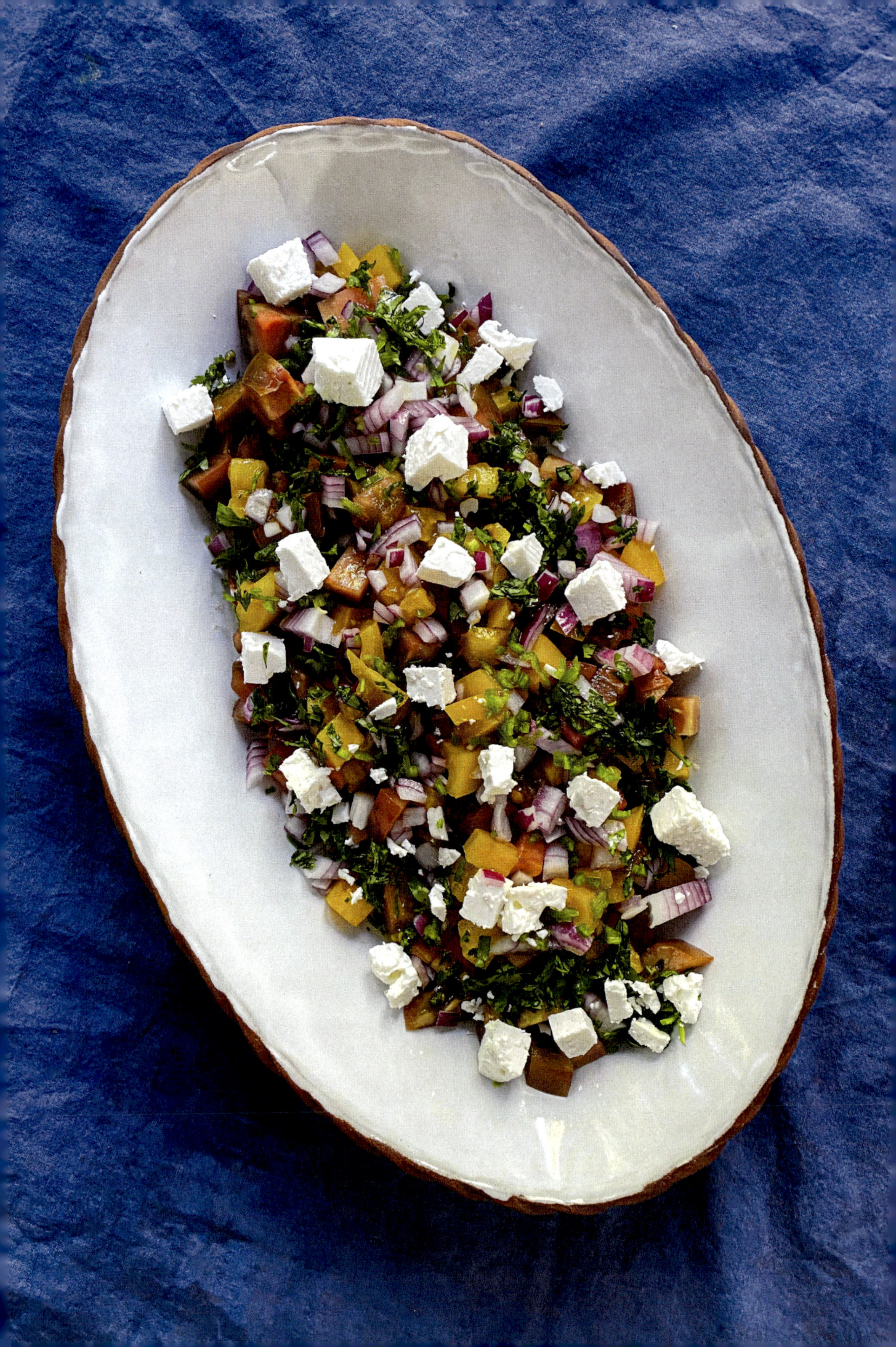

GREEK-ISH SALAD

4 large heirloom tomatoes or 8 regular tomatoes, diced

1 small red onion, diced small

1 green chile, diced small

¼ cup finely chopped parsley

2 oz. feta or vegan feta cheese, diced

A generous splash of olive oil

2 tablespoons fresh lemon juice

1 tablespoon chopped mint leaves

Salt

Pepper

Nowadays everything is always available, including heirloom tomatoes. So you can prepare this salad anytime of the year. However, the best time to make it is summer, when tomatoes are in season, and mint is cooling.

MAKES 4 SERVINGS

1 Combine the first 8 ingredients in a bowl.

2 Season to taste with salt and pepper, and toss well.

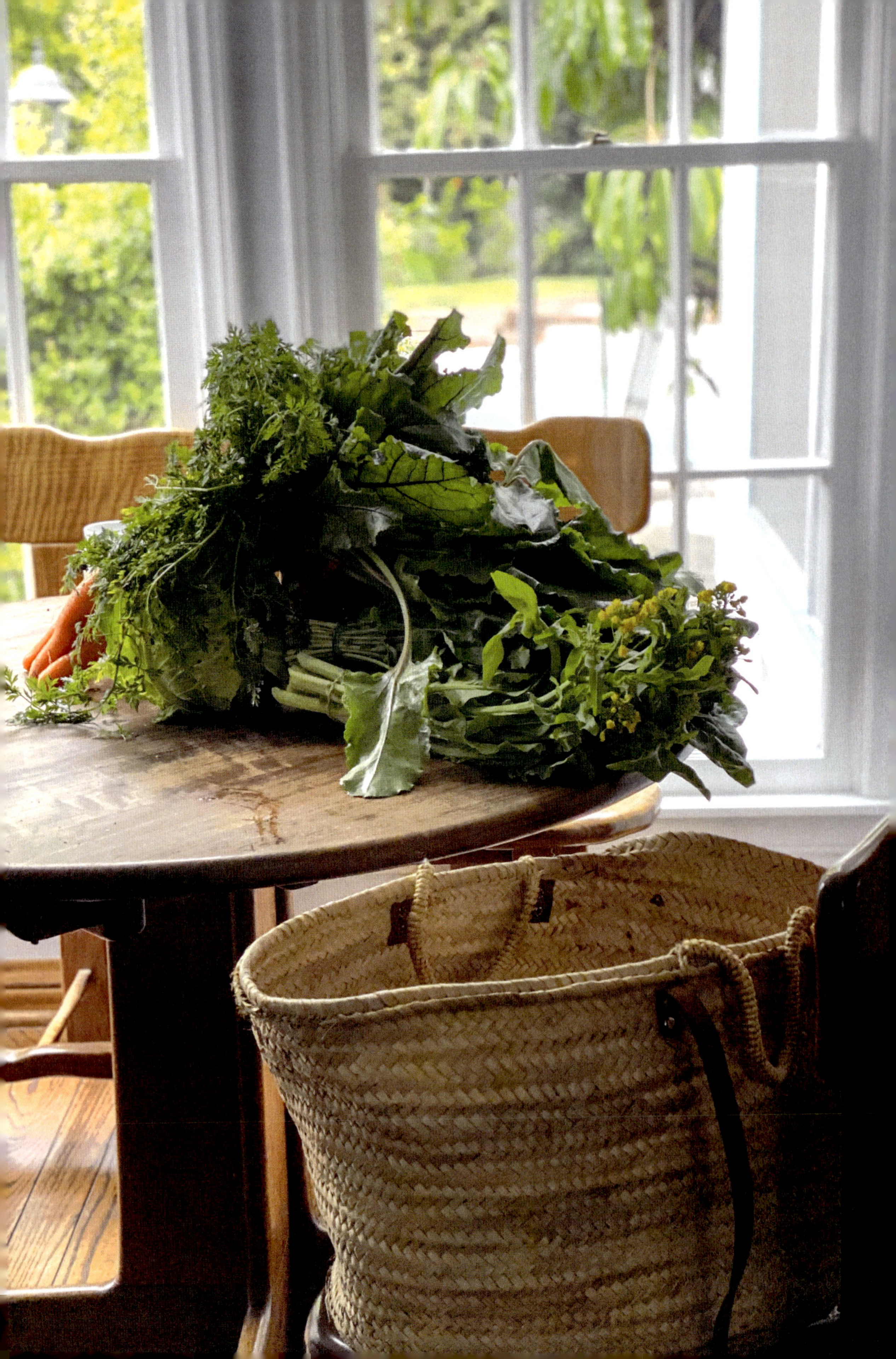

CHAPTER TWO

JIFFY LEAFY

When I was a kid in Israel, there wasn't a large selection of leafy greens like we have now. And the leafy greens we had were Swiss chard, beet leaves and collard greens, which we only ate in cooked salads. The green salad that we lived on was simple romaine with olive oil, lemon juice, salt and pepper.

Now even though there's an abundance to choose from, romaine remains my favorite. I love its crunchy, sweet spine and those thin, mildly grassy leaves. No wonder kids love it too. When my boys were toddlers, I would place a plate of fresh romaine leaves on the coffee table, as if they were cookies. Just left them there without saying a word. Ten seconds later, I would hear that satisfying kch kch. They always devoured them like hungry caterpillars. That's why romaine features prominently in this chapter.

Fresh romaine leaves are shiny and the spine is perky like my breast was up until I had kids. When the head of lettuce is beautiful and vibrant, I let it shine solo in a salad. But if it's tired and bitter like a desperate housewife, I Wim-Hof it up by soaking it in ice-cold water and chop the leaves finely so they absorb the dressing, and I add other vegetables and a crunchy fruit such as apple.

Feel free to use any lettuce or mixed greens that you like. Though if you're going for tough leaves like kale, I recommend steaming them for a couple of minutes or chopping the leaves up nice and thin. That way, they'll absorb the dressing and soften up. Remember, if it's hard to chew, it's hard to digest. We're not cows, we don't have four stomachs. Our stomach needs a little help breaking down thick leaves.

HOW TO TELL IF YOUR GREENS ARE FRESH:

- You want the greens to be a vibrant, rich green. If you've got red or purple lettuce in the mix, look for a deep, purplish hue that screams, "I'm fresh!" If the lettuce looks dull, yellowing, or has brown edges, have compassion but walk away.

- Give that lettuce a gentle squeeze. If it's crisp, go for it. If it's limp or wilted, no good.

- Fresh lettuce should have a mild, slightly sweet aroma that's pleasant and inviting. If you're getting strong, funky, or musty smells, that lettuce is no longer fresh.

- Watch out for any accumulated moisture or condensation on the inside of the packaging. That's a sign that the lettuce is starting to decompose, and you don't want to eat it.

- Check for brown spots or rusty-looking edges on the leaves. If you see any of that, it's a clear indication of decay, and that lettuce is no longer fresh.

- Take a look at the stem ends where the lettuce was cut. They should look freshly trimmed, not dried out, brownish, or oxidized.

NOTES:

- If you want to make your green salad more exciting, add toasted nuts and/or seeds for a boost of umami goodness. And don't be afraid to throw in some crunchy fruits and vegetables like apples, pears, fennel, beets, and carrots; julienned, so they soak the dressing and also are easier to chew.

- Unless you're into entomophagy (eating bugs) or love the texture of sand, you should wash your greens. And when I say wash, I mean soak them in cold water for at least five minutes. Pre-washed or not, I soak my greens in cold water in a salad spinner—the only kitchen gadget I cannot live without. If you're dealing with clingy, persistent little bugs (aphids) that won't let go, add a tablespoon of salt or a couple of tablespoons of white vinegar to the soaking water. It won't affect the flavor or the nutritional value. Once you've given your greens a good soak, spin and dry them. If you don't own a salad spinner, dry them on a clean white kitchen towel.

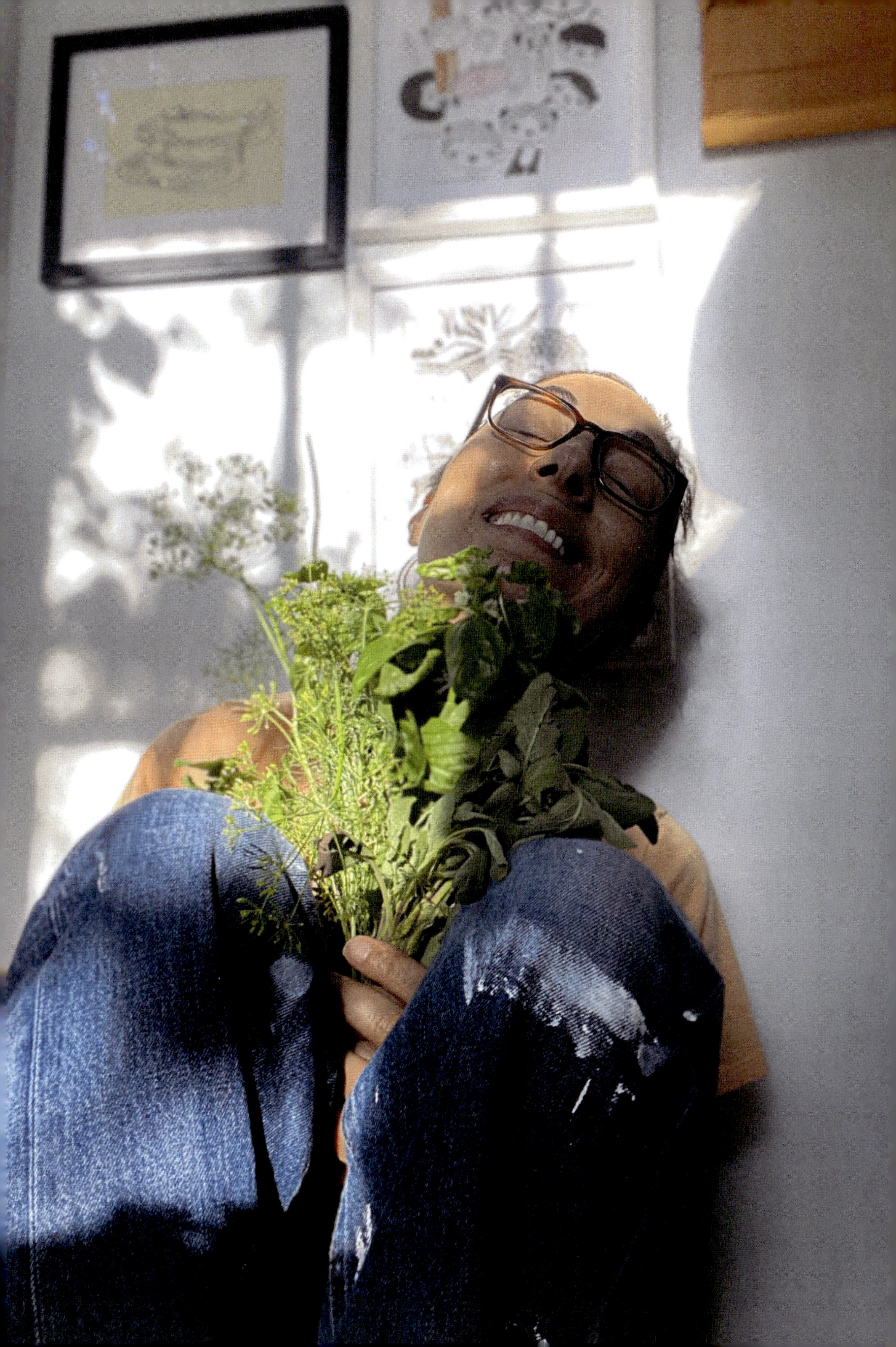

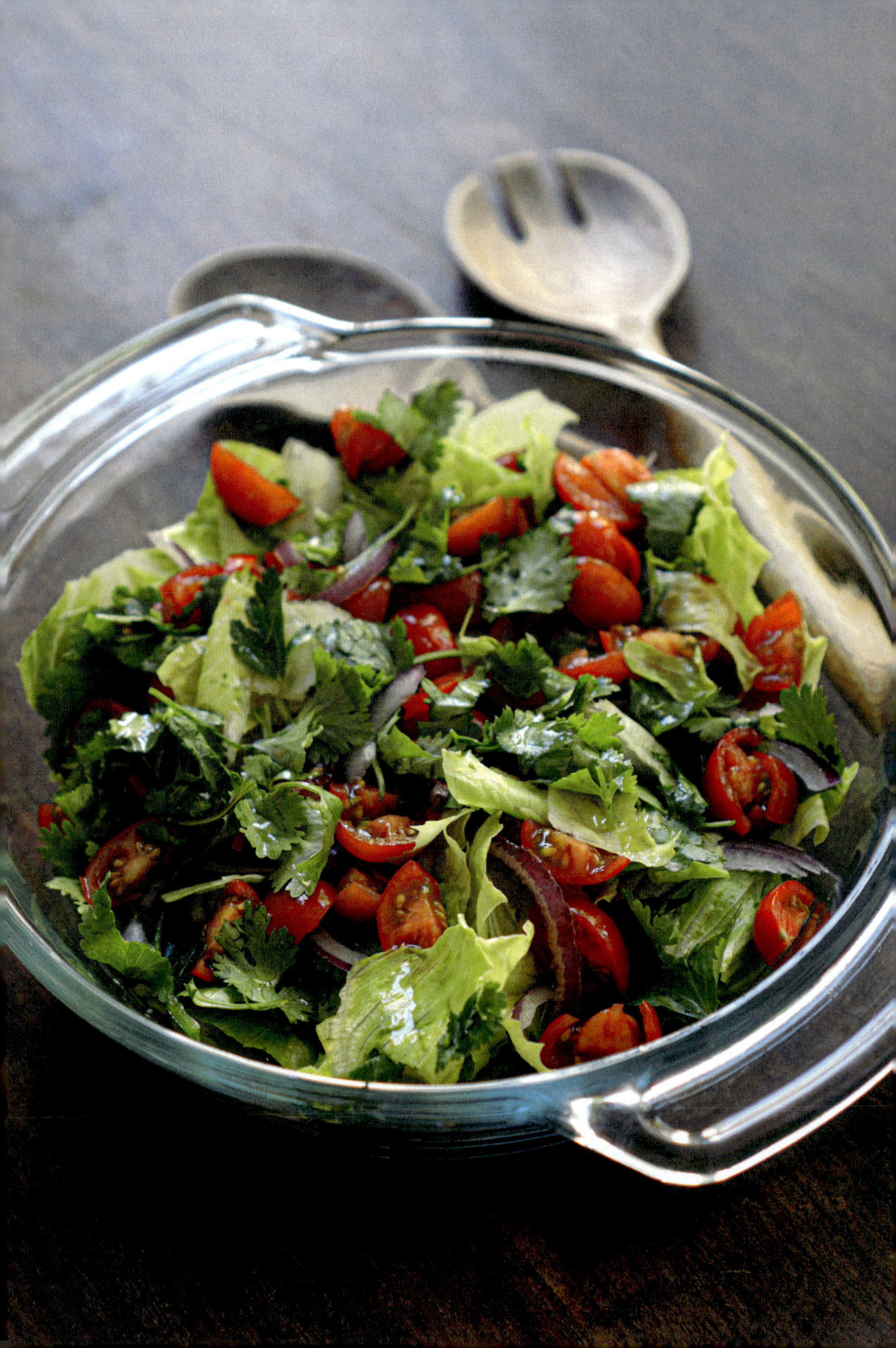

SALAT ESTEE

4 romaine lettuce leaves, chopped roughly

5 cherry tomatoes, sliced in half or quartered

Small red onion, sliced (optional)

1 small green pepper, chopped roughly (optional)

Handful cilantro leaves

1 tablespoon olive oil

1 tablespoon lemon juice

Salt

Black pepper

Estee, my mother-in-law, rarely cooks. You'll never see her stirring a pot or getting something out of the oven. She eats most of her meals out, but when she does eat at home, it would be light and an assembly of good bread, some cheese, olives and this salad.

NOTES:

❖ You can make this salad with parsley instead of cilantro.

❖ In the summer you can add a few mint leaves to make it even more refreshing and cooling. Just stack them together and chop them or cut them with scissors.

❖ If you would like to use onion but don't know what to do with the rest of it, cure it with salt and lemon juice and use it during the week—peel the onion, cut it in half and slice thin. Put it in a jar or container with 1 tablespoon lemon juice or apple cider vinegar, ½ teaspoon salt and 1 tablespoon sumac (optional) and toss well. Keep in the fridge up to a week. Add to salads or sandwiches.

MAKES 1 SERVING

Combine the first 7 ingredients, season to taste with salt and pepper and toss well.

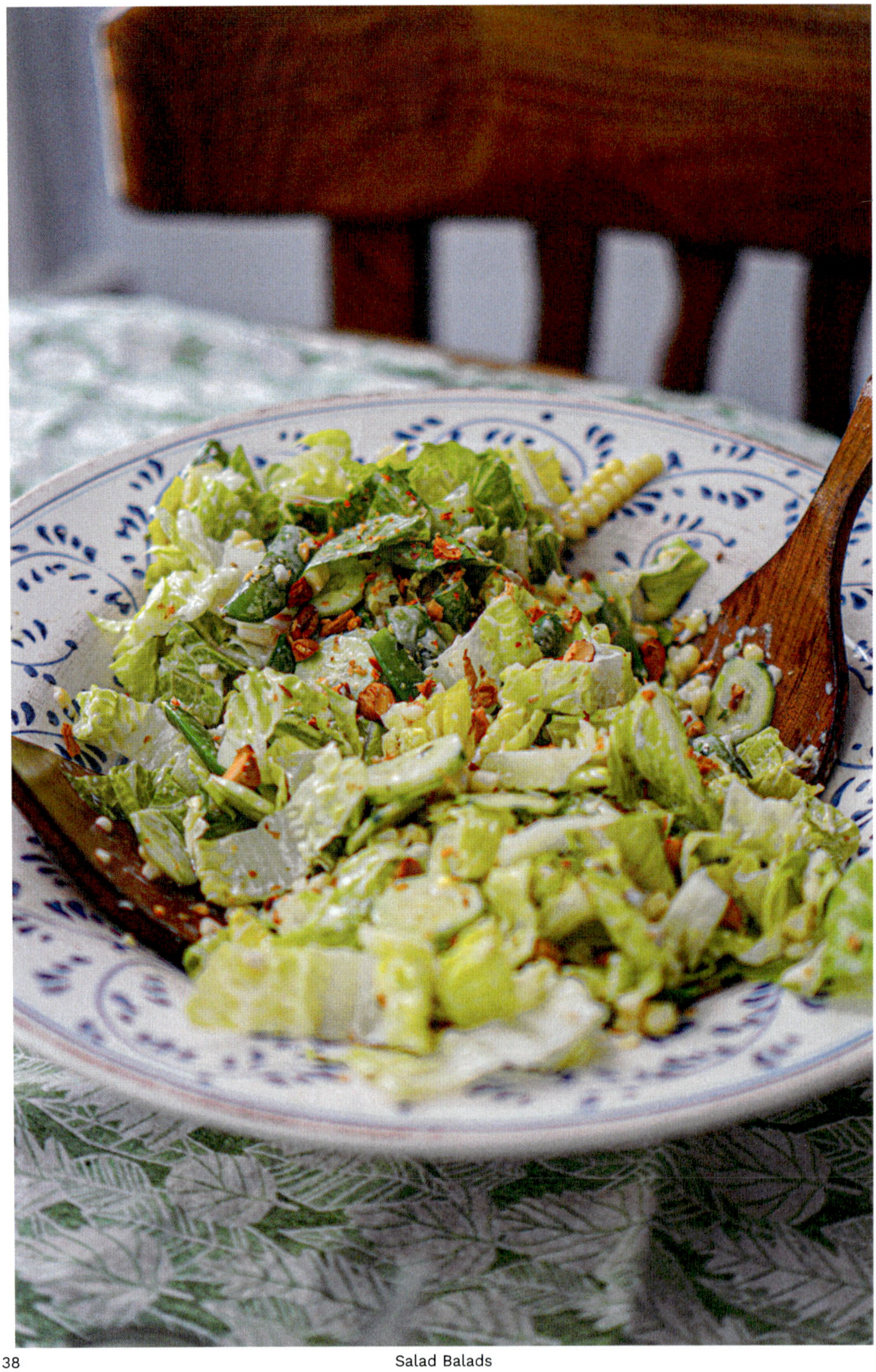

LETTUCE, CORN, CUCUMBER & SNAP PEAS

15 large romaine lettuce leaves, chopped

2 Persian cucumbers, cut lengthwise in half and sliced

2 cups cooked corn kernels

2 cups snap peas, thinly sliced

½ cup toasted almonds, chopped

¼ cup olive oil

¼ cup fresh lemon juice

1 teaspoon apple cider vinegar Salt

Salt

Pepper

This is one of my signature salads. No matter how big I make it, there are never any leftovers. If corn is not in season, feel free to use canned corn.

MAKES 4 SERVINGS

1 Put the 5 first ingredients in a bowl.

2 Put the olive, lemon juice, apple cider in a jar or a bowl and shake or whisk vigorously. Taste and add salt if needed. Pour the dressing over the salad and toss well. Serve immediately.

Salad Balads

ARUGULA, CUCUMBER, HARD-BOILED EGG & CROUTONS OVER TAHINI

CROUTONS

3 slices stale or frozen sourdough bread

A generous splash of olive oil

2 teaspoons za'atar

TAHINI

¼ cup or more tahini

2 tablespoons fresh lemon juice

¼ cup or more water

DRESSING

1 tablespoon olive oil

1 tablespoon fresh lemon juice

1 teaspoon apple cider vinegar

Salt

Pepper

SALAD

4 Persian cucumbers, chopped

2 hard-boiled eggs, quartered (optional)

2 scallions, chopped

1 red bell pepper, seeded, deveined and chopped

1 handful arugula or mixed greens, chopped

Long ingredient list, but most items are pantry staples you most likely have on hand.

Whenever I have random bits and pieces of stale bread, frozen bread, or baguette ends lying around the freezer, I make this salad. Croutons are like savory cereal chunks—they soak up the dressing and slightly soften but at the same time keep that satisfying crunch.

MAKES 4 SERVINGS

1. To make the croutons: Preheat the oven or toaster oven to 350°F (175°C). Place bread slices on a baking tray and drizzle with olive oil. Sprinkle 2 teaspoons of za'atar seasoning, salt, and pepper. Bake for 10 minutes or until toasted but not overly hard.

2. To make the tahini: In a small bowl, whisk together the tahini, remaining 2 tablespoons lemon juice, and ¼ cup water until smooth and well-combined. If the tahini is too thick, add more water, 1 teaspoon at a time. If it's too runny, add a spoon or two of tahini.

3. To make the dressing: Whisk the olive oil, lemon juice and vinegar in a large salad bowl until combined. Season with salt and pepper.

4. To make the salad: Add all the salad ingredients into the dressing bowl and toss well.

5. Spread 2 spoonful tahini on a dip plate or in a small bowl. Top with a portion of salad and sprinkle as many croutons you like over.

Ballad of Salad

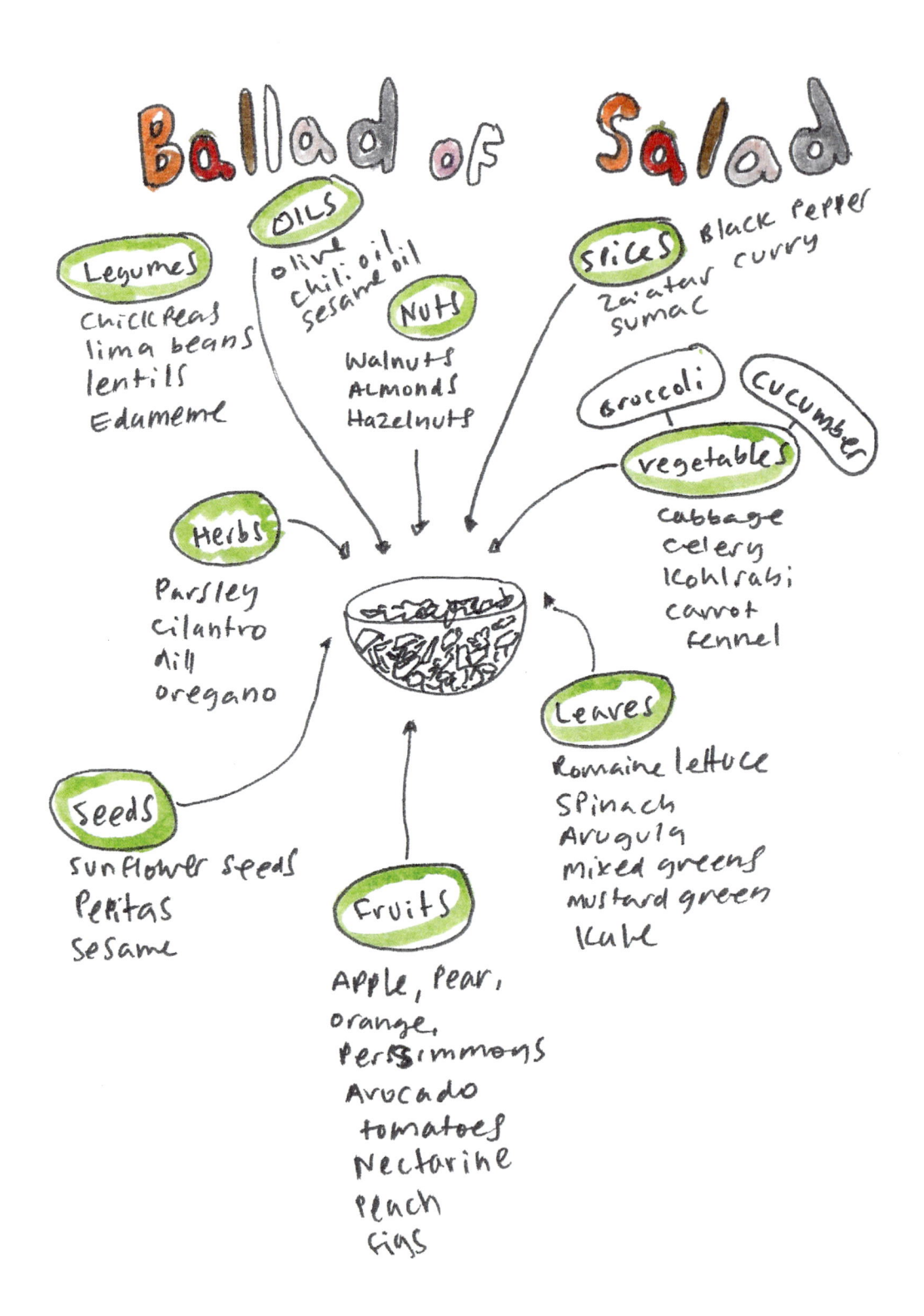

Legumes
Chickpeas
lima beans
lentils
Edameme

Oils
olive oil
chili oil
sesame oil

Nuts
Walnuts
Almonds
Hazelnuts

Spices
Black pepper
Za'atar
curry
sumac

Broccoli

Cucumber

Vegetables
cabbage
celery
kohlrabi
carrot
fennel

Herbs
Parsley
cilantro
dill
oregano

Leaves
Romaine lettuce
Spinach
Arugula
mixed greens
mustard green
Kale

Seeds
sunflower seeds
Pepitas
Sesame

Fruits
Apple, Pear,
orange,
Persimmons
Avocado
tomatoes
Nectarine
Peach
Figs

Salad Balads

JIFFY LEAFY

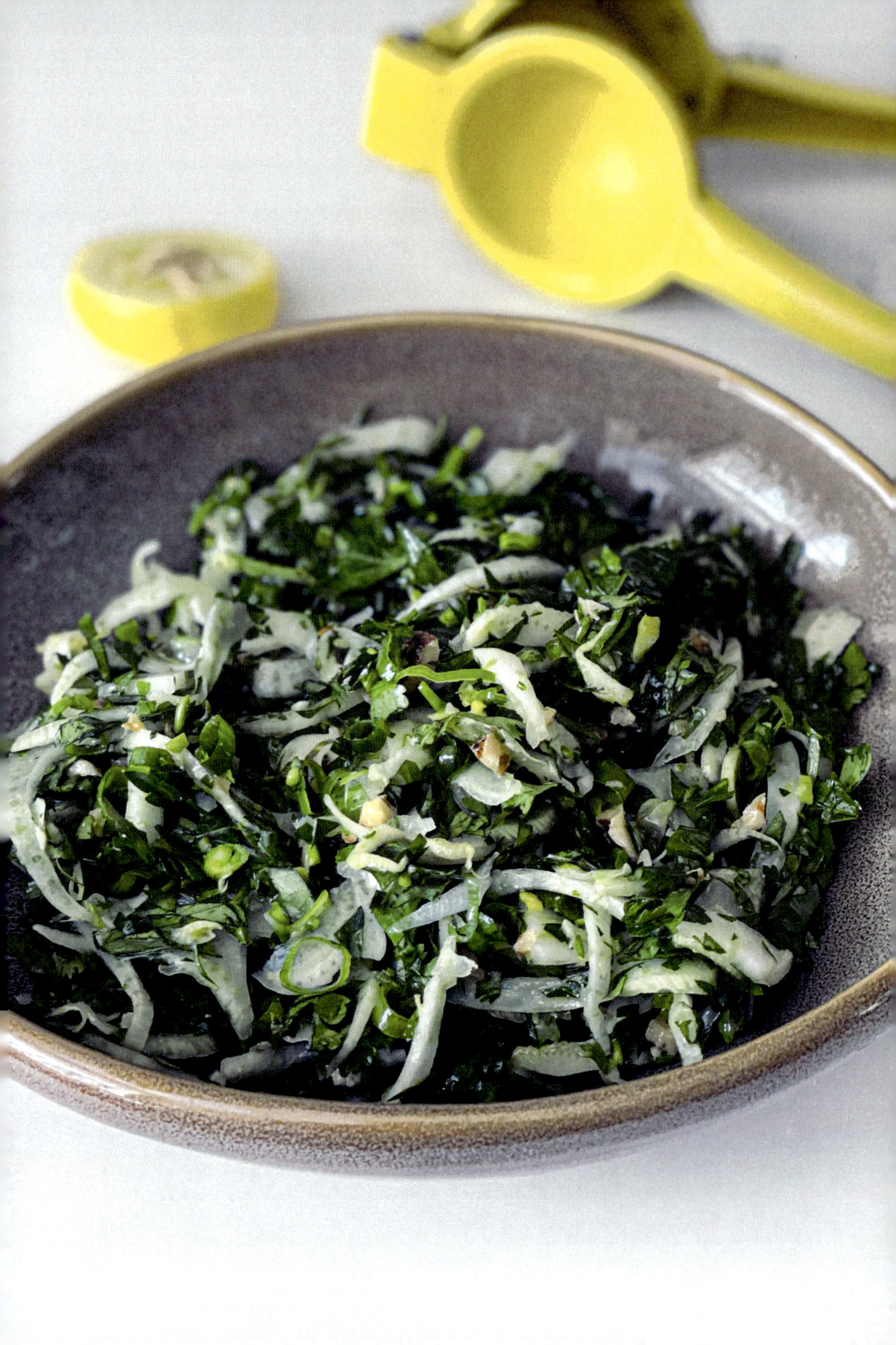

WEDDING HERB SALAD

1 fennel bulb, trimmed and sliced thinly

1 teaspoon coarse salt or ½ teaspoon or more table salt

1 cup cilantro, chopped finely

1 cup parsley, chopped finely

4 scallions, only green part (save the whites for another dish), chopped finely

¼ cup walnuts, chopped roughly

3 tablespoons olive oil

**2 tablespoons or more fresh lemon juice
Pepper**

Pepper

This salad was served at both of my sisters' weddings. My eldest sister said that this salad stars in weddings in the Negev, the southern desert of Israel. People there love it. If I had a wedding, I would have probably also had it on the menu. But I would have had add crunchy shaved fennel to mine.

MAKES 4 SERVINGS

1. Put the fennel in a medium salad bowl, sprinkle the salt on and massage it.

2. Add the herbs, olive oil and lemon juice, season with black pepper and toss well.

3. Taste and if necessary add salt, olive oil or lemon juice. Serve immediately or refrigerate for 2 days.

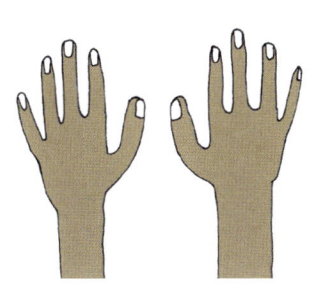

The ultimate tongs

CHAPTER THREE

TUTTI-FRUTTI

When I was growing up, the only sweet and savory salad I knew was my grandmother's orange, fennel, black olive, and harissa salad. Sometimes I wonder why my mother and grandmother didn't add other fruits to their salads. Except for bananas, I'm open to trying any fruit in my salad, as long as it has a tang.

In early summer, when stone fruits are in season and still firm, I like to add them to salads. I love the combination of sweet and tender nectarines or plums with crunchy celery or kohlrabi. During winter, I mix oranges or pomelo in my Waldorf. In the fall, I add persimmons to my root salads. For me, one or two chopped fruits provide enough sweetness to a salad for four people.

You can make the salads in this chapter year-round by substituting the fruit based on what's in season. If persimmons aren't available, use a peach or apple instead. If you're unsure about a particular combination, cut a small piece of the fruit and a small piece of the vegetable and taste them together to see how they get along in your mouth. One of the aims of this book is to encourage you to create your own versions and help you to become a salad monster and master.

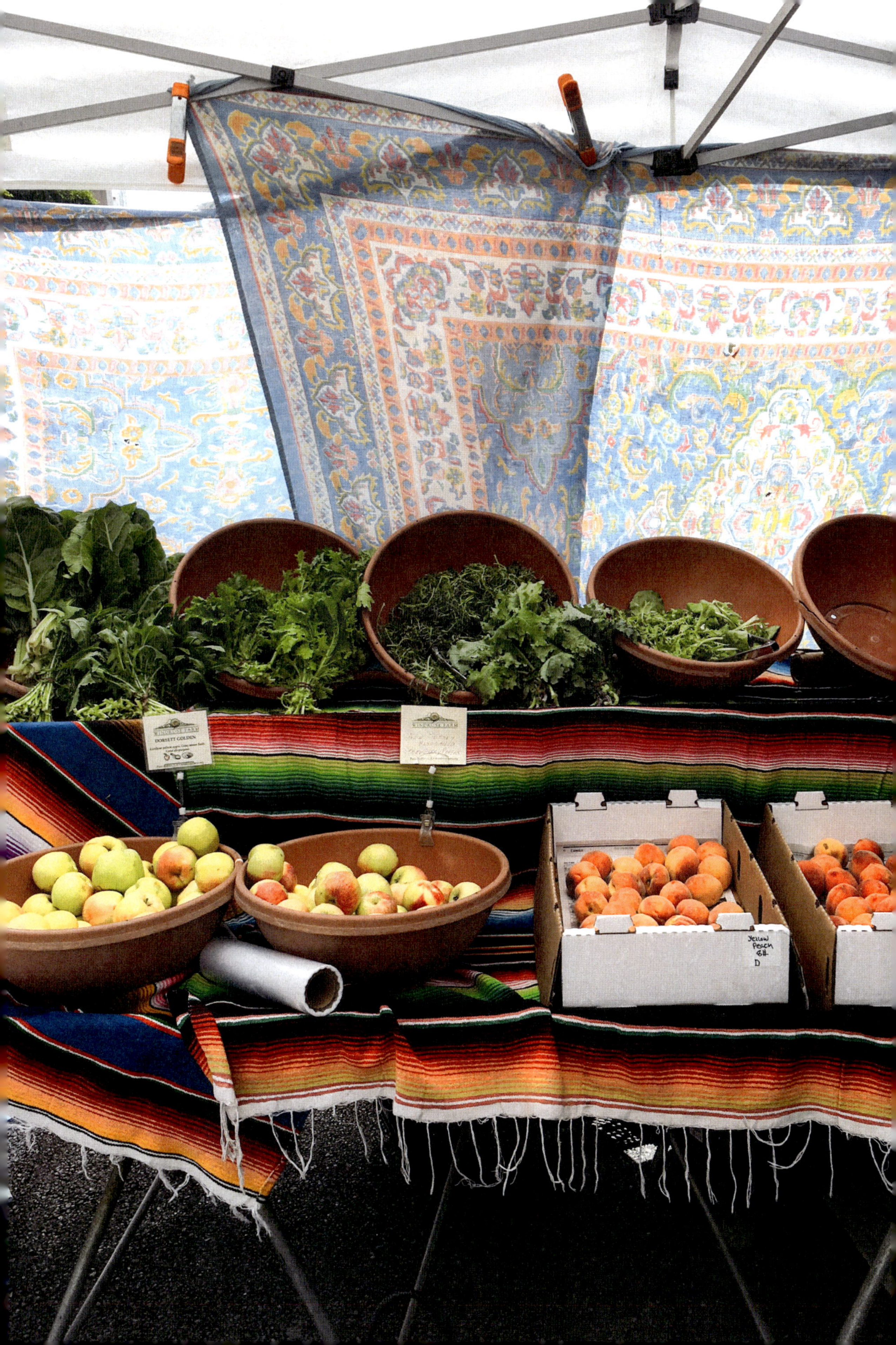
DORSETT GOLDEN
Yellow
Peach
8#
D

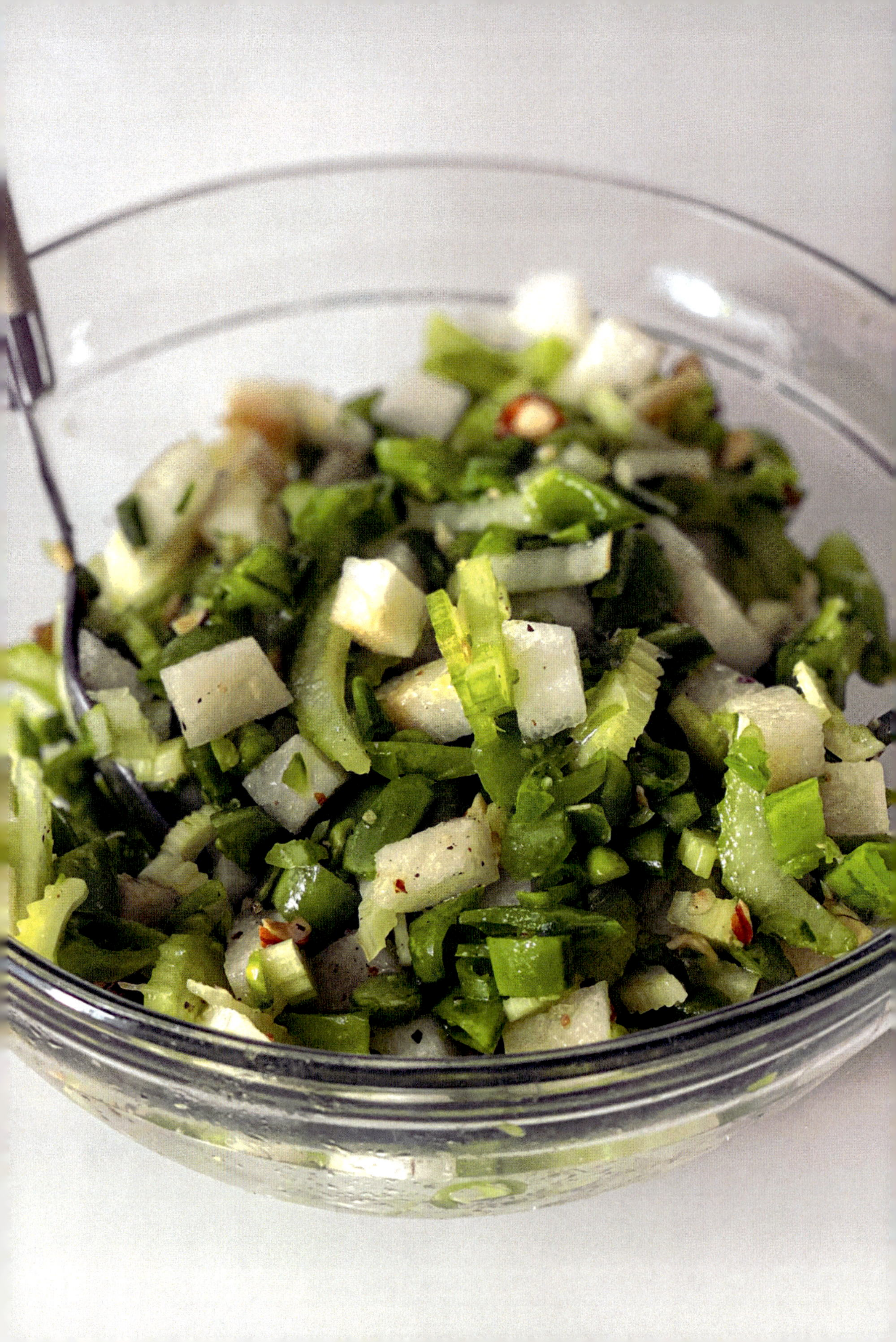

ASIAN PEAR, CELERY, SNAP PEAS & TOASTED ALMONDS

6 celery sticks, thinly sliced

1 cup thinly sliced snap peas

1 large Asian pear or another crunchy fruit, diced

¼ cup toasted hazelnuts or any nuts, chopped

¼ cup lemon juice

2 tablespoons olive oil

1 teaspoon apple cider vinegar

Salt

Black pepper

I'm not kidding, I'm addicted to the combination of crunchy, earthy vegetables, sweet juicy fruits, and nuts. I could devour an entire bowl of this salad every day and never get tired of it. When you slice the snap peas they drink the tangy dressing, so don't consider keeping them whole.

NOTE:

- ❖ Any crunchy fruit would work in this salad.

MAKES 2 TO 4 SERVINGS

Combine the first 7 ingredients in a large bowl. Season to taste with salt and pepper and toss well.

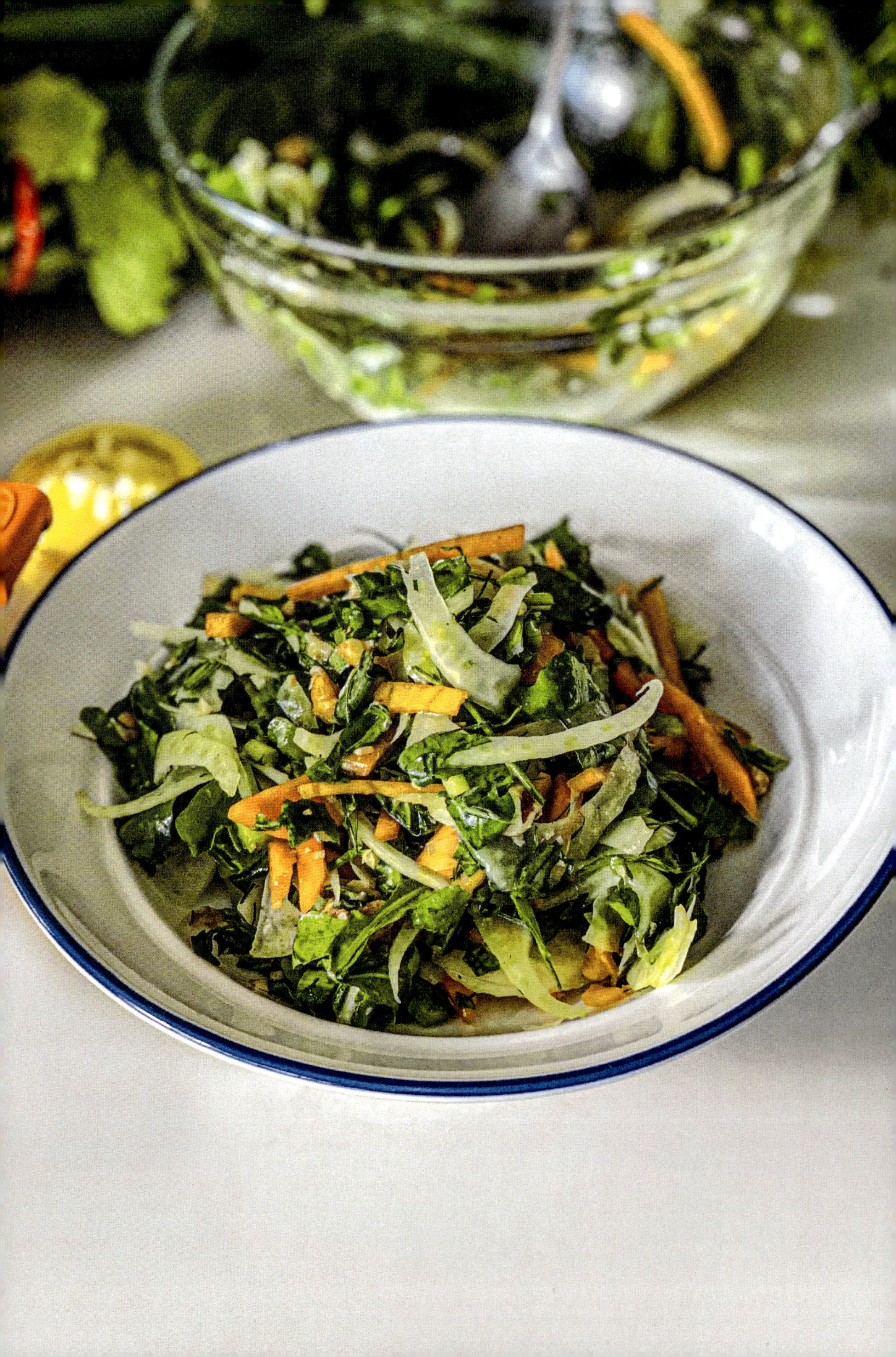

PHENOMENAL FENNEL, ARUGULA & PERSIMMON SALAD

1 firm Fuyu persimmon, peeled, pitted and julienned

1 medium fennel bulb, trimmed and sliced as thinly as possible

1 bunch of arugula, rinsed thoroughly and chopped

Handful walnuts or any other nut, chopped

3 tablespoons olive oil

2 tablespoons or more fresh lemon juice

Salt

Pepper

If you're looking to impress, make this salad. Not only is it good-looking, but it's gorgeous tasting. The combo of liquoricey fennel, sugary persimmons, spicy arugula, and acidic lemon juice is *fennomenal*.

NOTES:

❖ If you've got a Japanese mandoline handy, use it to shave the fennel super thin – it makes life easier. If you don't, no worry, a sharp knife will get the job done.

❖ When persimmons aren't in season, you can replace them with oranges, apples, or pears.

MAKES 2 TO 4 SERVINGS

1. Combine the persimmon, fennel, arugula and nuts in a large salad bowl.

2. Add olive oil, 2 tablespoons lemon juice and season to taste with salt and pepper.

3. Toss well, preferably, with your hands. Serve immediately.

BLOODY WALDORF SALAD

5 blood oranges or any kind orange, peeled and diced

4 celery sticks, thinly sliced

½ cup pecans, chopped

Handful cilantro or dill or both, chopped

Lemon zest from 1 lemon (optional)

2 tablespoons lemon juice

1 tablespoon mayonnaise or vegan mayonaise

1 tablespoon olive oil

Coarse salt

Black pepper

When I make this salad or even think about it, I think about my sister, Liraz. When we lived in New York, she used to make it every Friday for Shabbat dinner. She usually makes it with fresh or canned pineapple. I do too, but during the winter, I make it with blood oranges, when they are in season.

NOTE:

- ❖ This recipe works with almost any sweet and acidic fruits or citrus fruits such as pomelo.

MAKES 4 SERVINGS

Combine the first 8 ingredients in a large bowl, season to taste with salt and pepper, and toss well. Serve immediately or refrigerate up to 1 day.

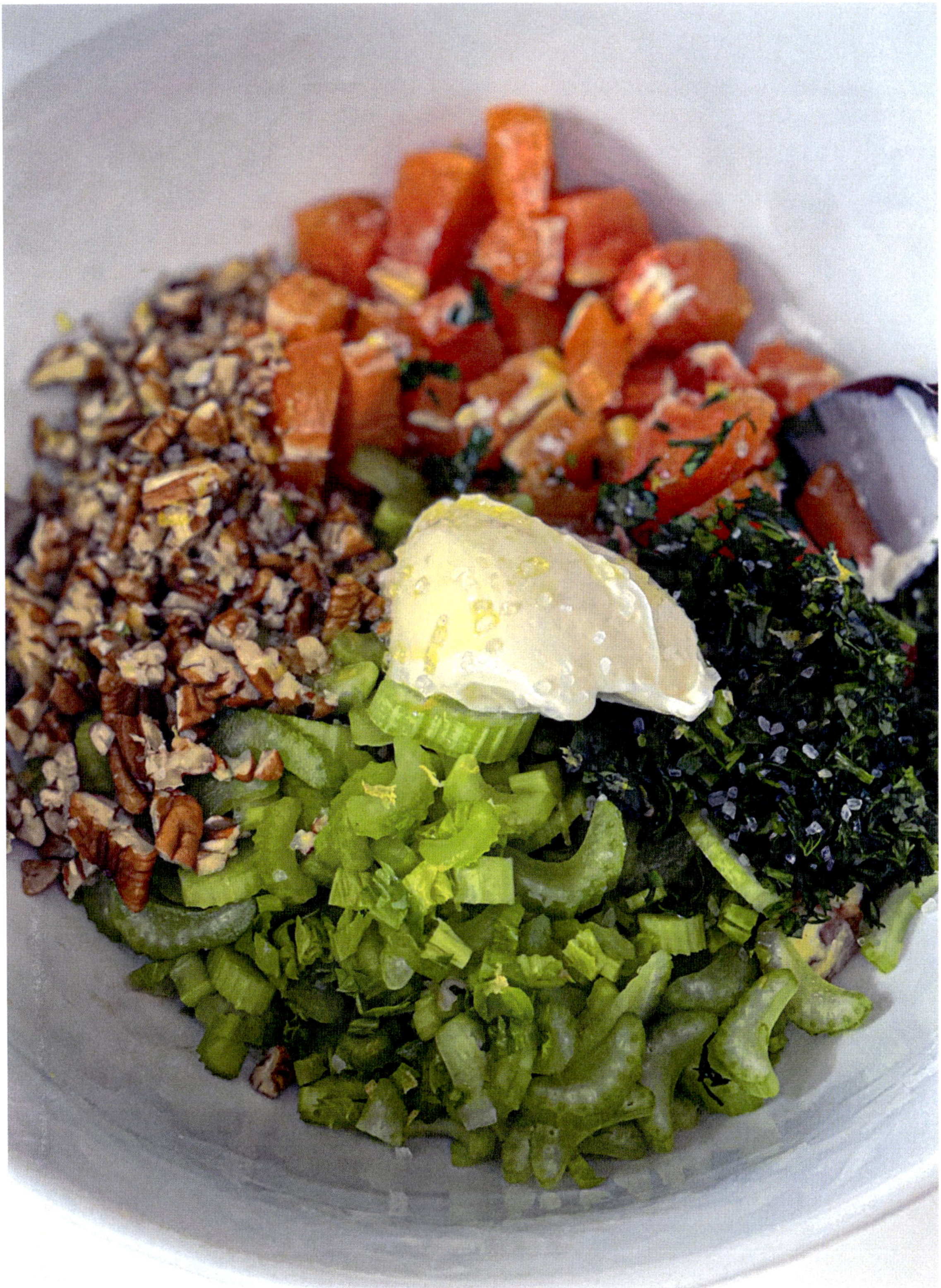

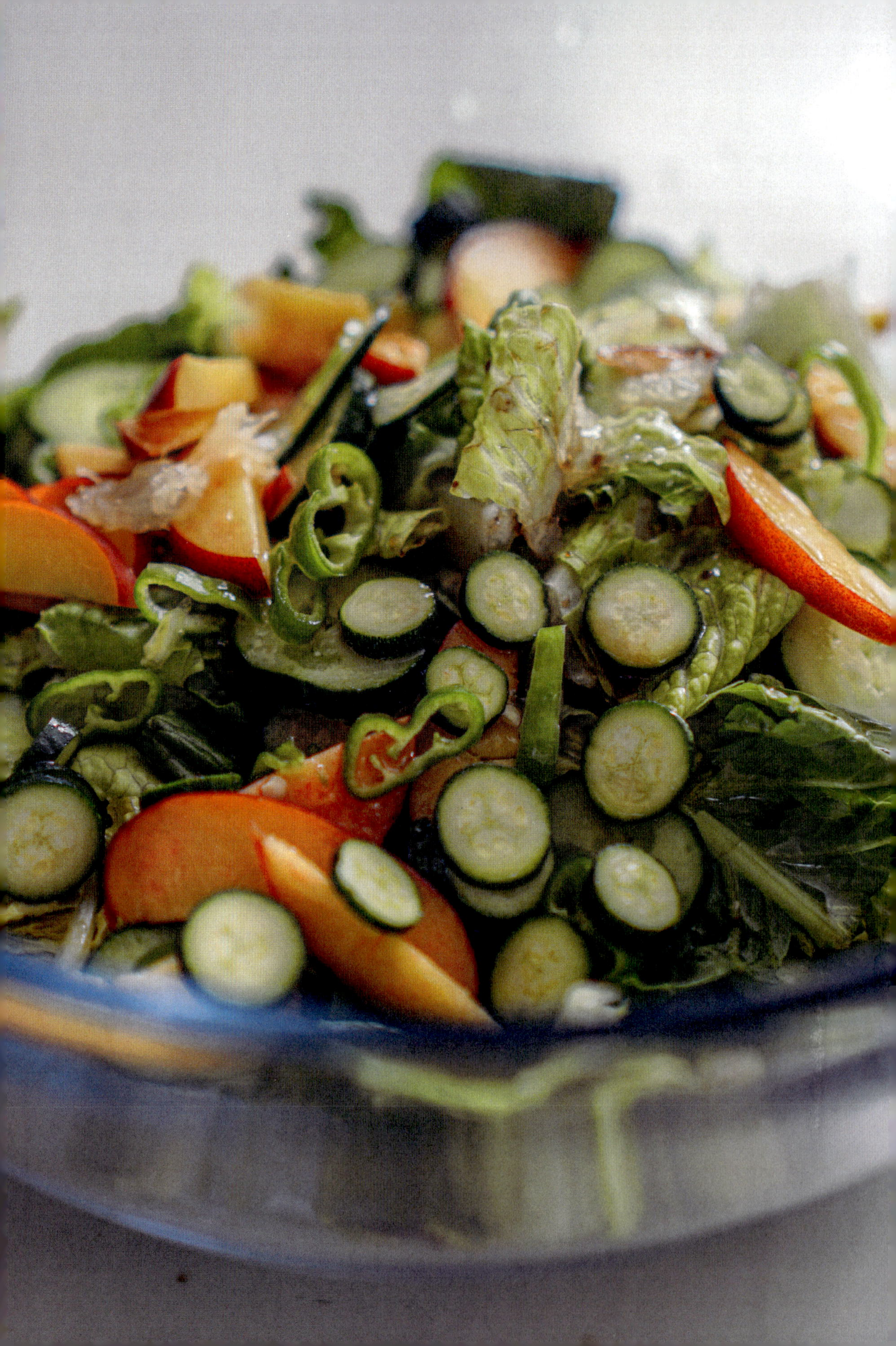

LETTUCE, ZUCCHINI & NECTARINE SALAD

SALAD

1 small head romaine lettuce

2 small zucchinis, sliced thinly

2 Korean green peppers or hatch chiles, sliced thinly - optional

2 medium nectarines, cut in half, seeded and sliced

DRESSING

¼ cup olive oil

1 teaspoon balsamic vinegar

Pinch of ground cinnamon

½ teaspoon salt

¼ teaspoon black pepper

Another simple salad that wows people with the combo of crisp vegetables and sweet soft fruits. The cinnamon in the dressing is what gets everyone curious - they can't quite place it, but they know something's different. I've seen people take a bite, pause, then go back for more trying to figure out what that kick is. I didn't come up with that brilliant addition; I learned it in New York, at Cafe Gitane in Nolita. They added cinnamon to their salad dressing, and I've been using their trick ever since.

NOTE:

❖ You can use a different type of pepper or skip the peppers.

❖ You can make the salad with another kind of stone fruit or any crunchy tart fruit.

MAKES 4 SERVINGS

1 Soak the romaine leaves in cold water for 10 minutes. Drain and dry in a salad spinner or with a clean kitchen towel. Slice the leaves or tear them with your hands and put in a large salad bowl.

2 Add the rest of the salad ingredients to the bowl.

3 Put the dressing ingredients in a small jar and cover it with a lid, shake vigorously.

4 Pour the dressing over the salad only when you are ready to eat. If you make the dressing ahead, store it in the fridge. Taste and add salt if necessary.

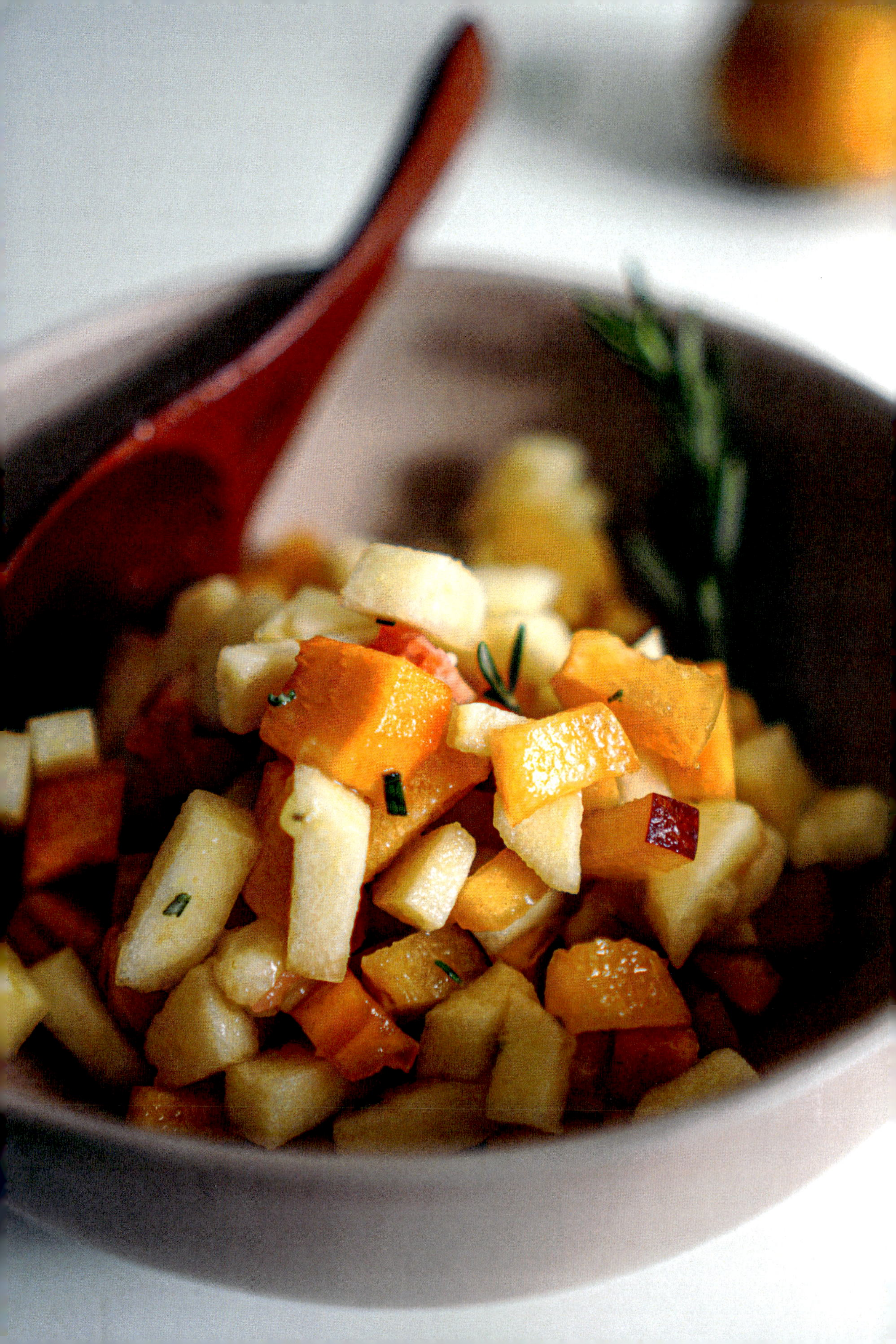

WINTER FRUIT SALAD

6 oranges, 4 peeled and diced, 2 juiced

4 medium any apples, peeled, cored and diced

4 Fuyu persimmons, peeled, cored and diced

3 small Asian pears or any pears, peeled, cored and diced

2 bananas, peeled and diced

½ teaspoon minced fresh rosemary (about 1 sprig, 15 leaves

Up until I was introduced to the combination of fruits and rosemary at Sage Vegan Bistro in Silver Lake, it didn't occur to me that rosemary could work in non-savory dishes. A decade later, it's now obvious. I add it to cakes, ice creams, and in the winter, to fruit salads. The earthy flavor of rosemary combined with sweet fruits is unexpected and delightful.

NOTES:

- I strongly recommend using fresh rosemary but If you only have dry rosemary, crush it into a powder and add only a pinch.
- Any type of apples work in this salad.
- Dice the oranges last, as they will make your cutting board wet. To minimize the number of dishes you need to wash, you can squeeze them directly into the salad bowl.

MAKES 4 SERVINGS

1 Combine the diced oranges, apples, persimmons, pears, bananas and minced rosemary in a large salad bowl.

2 Add the juice from the 2 squeezed oranges and toss well. Serve immediately or refrigerate for up to 2 days.

TUTTI-FRUTTI

CHAPTER FOUR

THE SCENIC ROOTS

Root salads are in my roots. Moroccan Jews can't sit down to eat if there isn't at least one root vegetable on the table. My grandmother served radishes or kohlrabi submerged in salted water with every meal. My father prepares a big container of his root vegetable salad weekly and keeps it in the fridge, ready for when he sits down to eat. Whenever I bump into fresh-looking, organic roots at the farmers market for a good price, I grab a bunch. They last pretty long.

If there were an Academy Award ceremony for vegetables, root vegetables would take home the Oscar for best performance and versatility, no question.

What is also great about them is that they last long because they contain high sugar content, which makes them appealing and delectable even for picky eaters. Especially when you marry them with sour flavors. So don't skip the lemon juice.

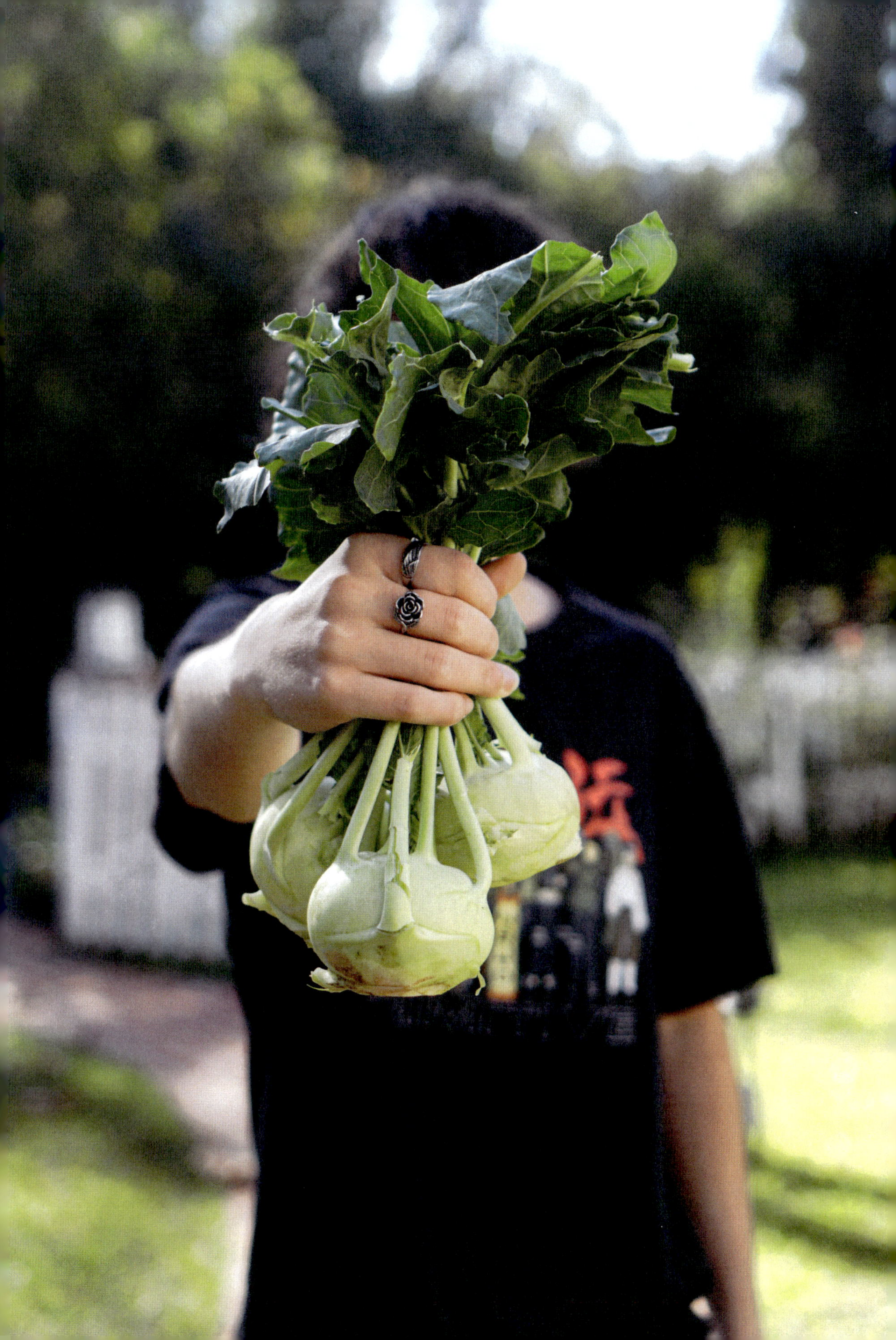

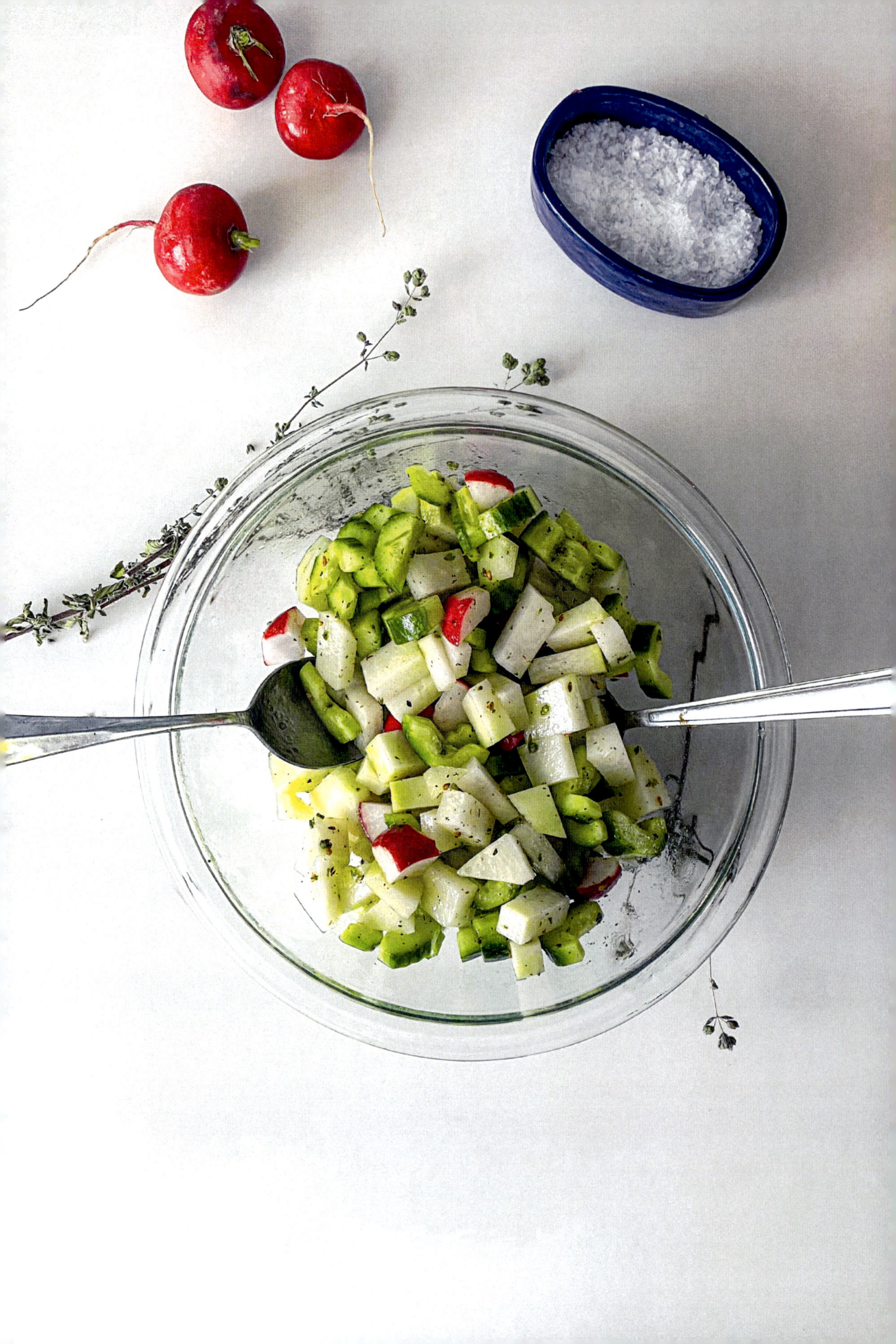

OUR EVERYDAY ROOT SALAD

1 large kohlrabi, peeled and diced

3 Persian cucumbers, diced

5 baby radishes, diced

½ teaspoon za'atar or fresh oregano leaves, chopped

1 tablespoon lemon juice

1 tablespoon oilve oil

Salt

Pepper

Don't be afraid of making a big batch of this salad—it won't last you long. And don't hold back on the lemon juice; it needs acidity like Los Angeles needs the rain.

NOTE:

❖ If you can't find kohlrabi, use jicama or young turnips for a similar crisp texture and mild sweetness.

MAKES 2 SERVINGS

Combine everything in a medium bowl, season with salt and pepper and toss well.

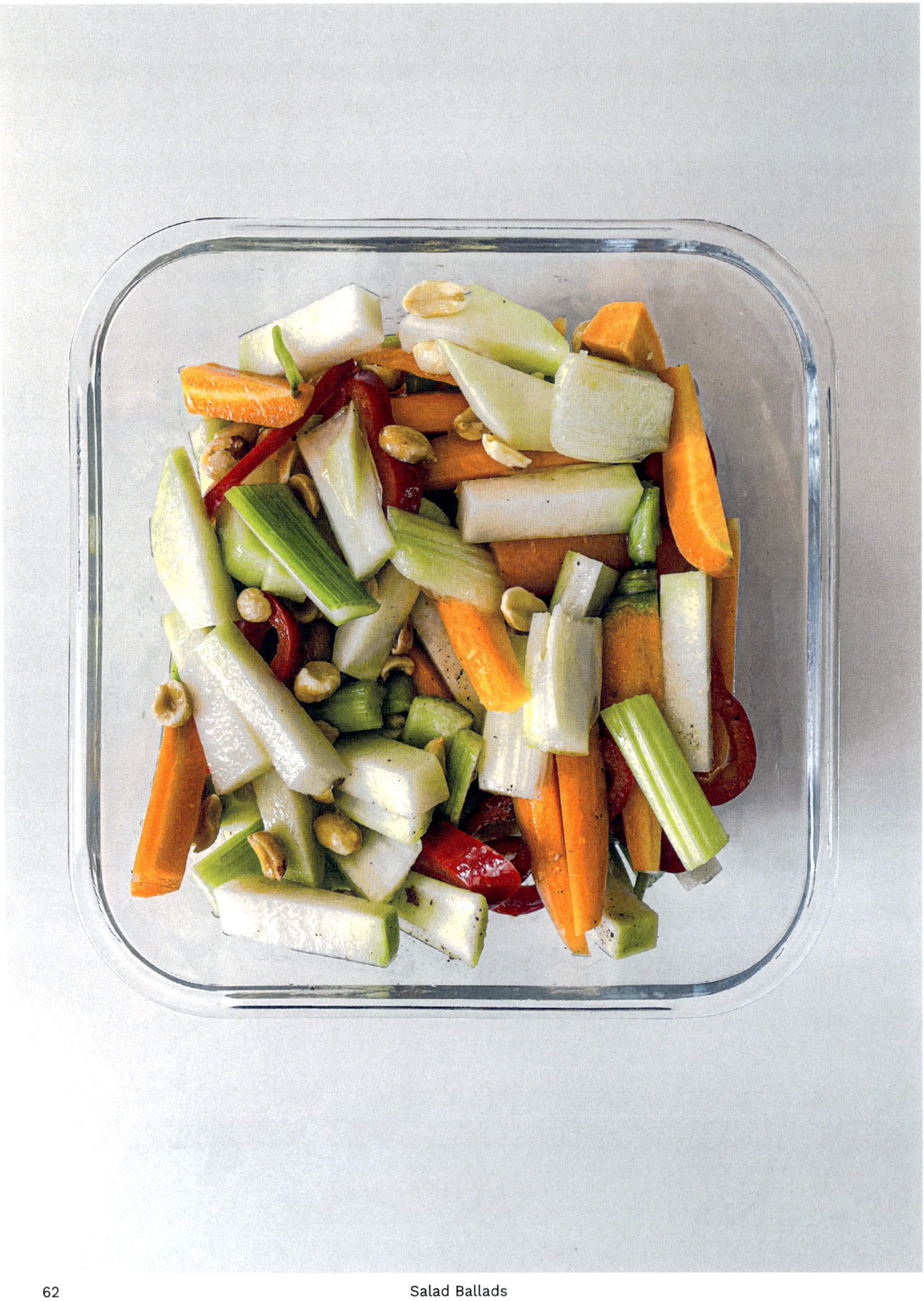

ABA'S QUICK-PICKLED ROOTS

4 medium carrots, peeled and cut into sticks

3 celery stalks, cut into sticks

1 large kohlrabi, cut into sticks

1 yellow, red or orange bell pepper, cut into sticks

¼ cup or more fresh lemon juice

2 tablespoons apple cider vinegar

2 tablespoons olive oil

Salt

Pepper

MAKES 4 TO 6 SERVINGS

1. Combine the vegetables, ¼ cup lemon juice, vinegar and olive oil in a large salad bowl, preferably one that comes with a lid.

2. Season with salt and pepper and toss well with your hands. Taste and add more lemon juice if desired. Serve immediately or keep in the fridge for up to 5 days.

Aba is "father" in Hebrew. My father makes a large jar of these quick pickles twice a week: Tuesdays, after he returns from the Shuk (market), and Fridays, for Shabbat. He eats a small plate of them with every meal. I make them when I buy too many root vegetables, and I binge on them when I am nervous or anxious, which is half of the time. Or when I travel. It's such a great nishnoosh (snack in Hebrew) to take on the plane. If you like add toasted nuts.

NOTES:

❖ You can make it with other vegetables such as fennel, baby radish, and raw cauliflower—chop it into small florets.

❖ Fresh lemon juice is a must. Not only does it bring out the natural sweetness of the vegetables, it also preserves them. You can use vinegar, but it would be too intense and might burn your throat. Limes would work, but the salad would have a different vibe.

❖ My dad seasons it with white pepper. It's got a milder, more earthy flavor than black pepper. I like it with either one.

❖ You can add toasted nuts and seeds such as almonds, walnuts and sunflower seeds.

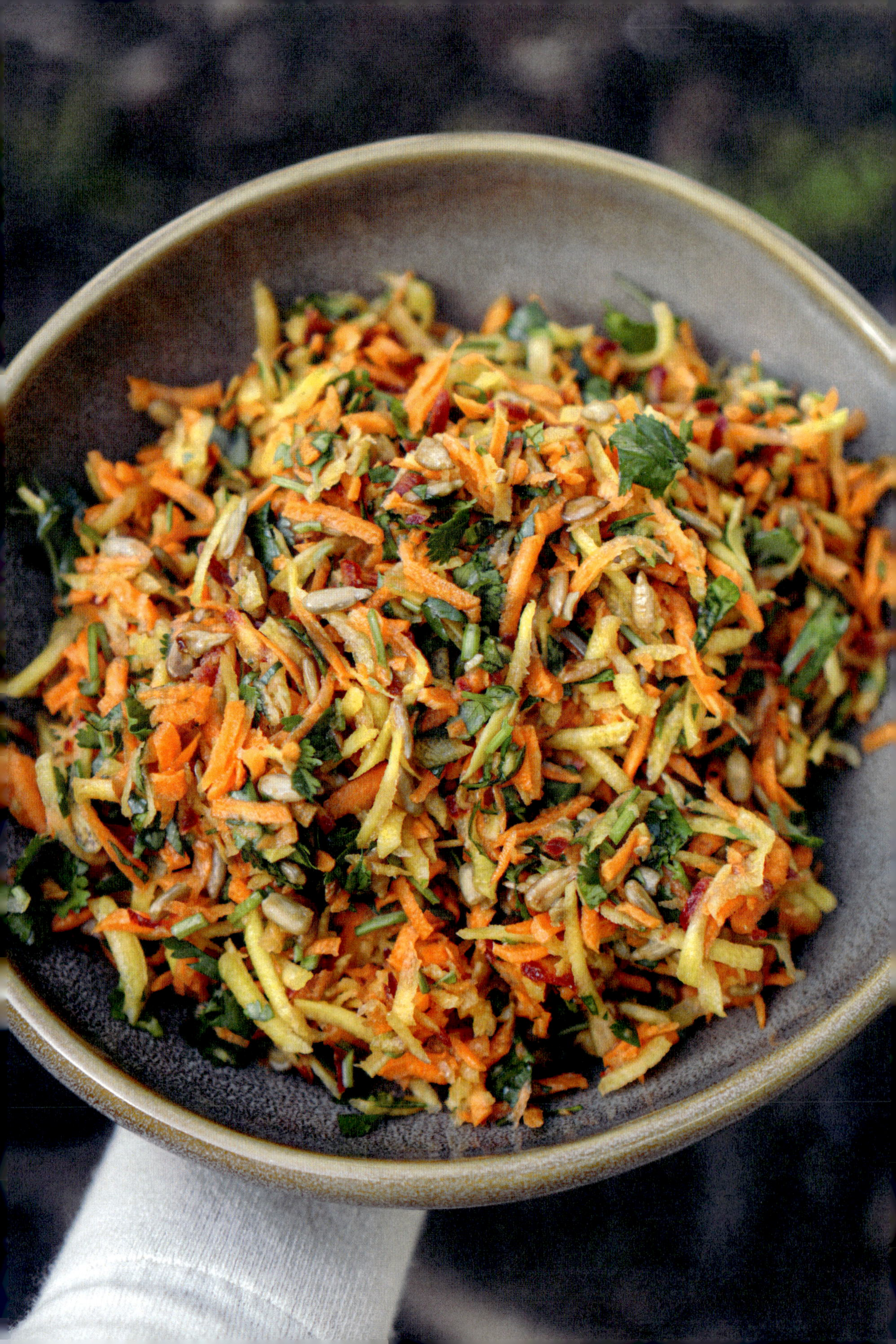

MAY THE BEST CARROT SALAD WIN

2 pounds carrots, peeled and grated

1 bunch cilantro or parsley or a combination of both, finely chopped (about ½ cup)

¼ cup toasted sunflower seeds or any other seeds or chopped nuts

¼ cup or more fresh lemon juice

2 tablespoons olive oil

1 tablespoon or more apple cider vinegar

Salt

Pepper

If there was a carrot salad competition, this salad would win without any doubt. You're going to thank me, just like I thanked my friend Sabrina, who introduced me to this budget-friendly, juicy, tangy, crowd-pleaser salad. Everyone loves it! Especially little ones and fussy eaters.

NOTE:

❖ 2 pounds of carrots is about 10 medium carrots.

❖ Sometimes I make it with different colors of carrots, but the flavor is just as good with regular carrots.

❖ Grate the carrots using the large holes of a box grater or with a food processor fitted with the disc blade attachment.

MAKES 4 SERVINGS

1. Combine carrots, cilantro, sunflower seeds, ¼ cup lemon juice, olive oil and 1 table apple cider vinegar in a large bowl.

2. Season to taste with salt and pepper and toss well, adding more lemon juice and apple cider vinegar if desired.

"Carrot cake, really? I prefer to be a salad"

CHAPTER FIVE

COOKED SALADS

For me, cooked salads are ba'eet (home in Hebrew), family, Friday noons, Shabbat. They symbolize abundance, dedication, and diligence—only when you prepare ten different types for Shabbat dinner and lunch, like my grandmother and mother did every week.

If the purpose of raw salads is to refresh, the purpose of cooked salads is to comfort. While most people serve cooked salads as an appetizer or side, I often add legumes and serve them as a main course.

Cooked salads are great when you're feeling low or under the weather, not only because they are comforting, but also because they are easier to digest and better for your immune system when it's fighting a disease.

Any roasted or steamed vegetable can transform into a refreshing salad. Simply dress it with lemon juice and mix in some chopped herbs.

I encourage you to play with the recipes below and experiment with different vegetables, grains, herbs, and nuts.

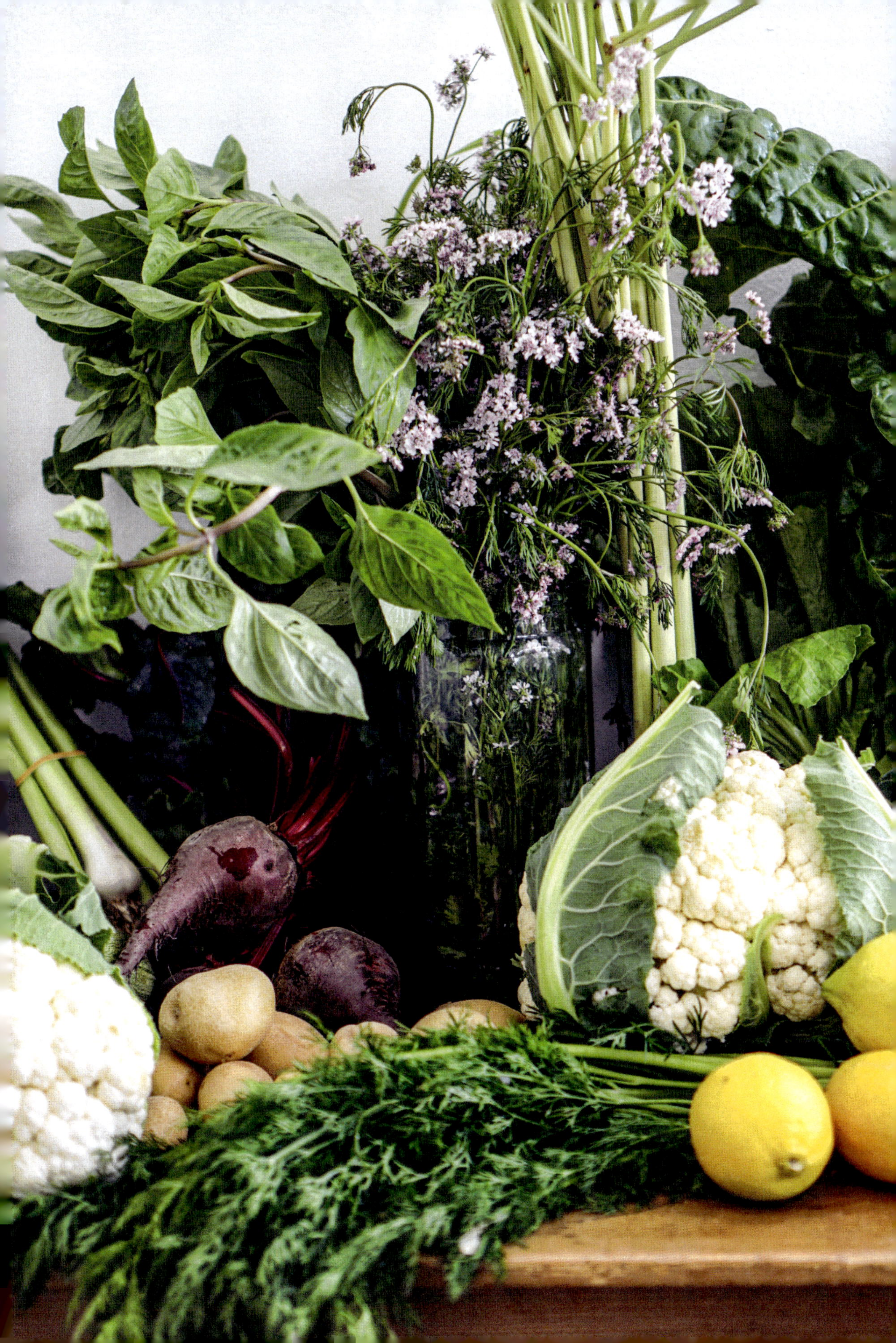

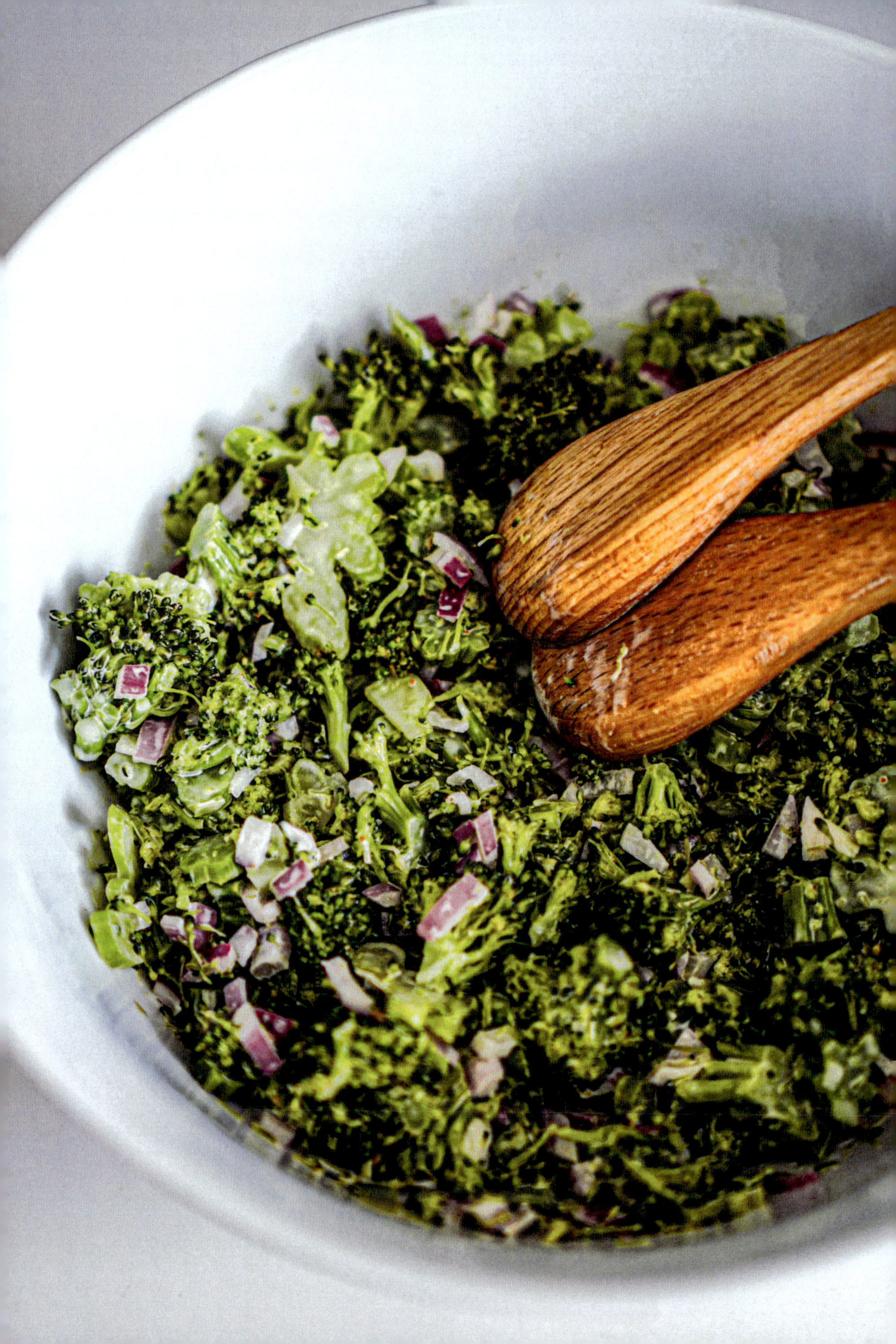

5-MINUTE BROCCOLI SALAD

1 broccoli head, separate the florets, peel the stem and slice it

DRESSING

¼ cup lemon juice

2 tablespoons mayonnaise or vegan mayonnaise

2 tablespoons olive oil

½ teaspoon curry powder

½ teaspoon salt

1 small red or white onion, finely sliced

I have to confess, broccoli doesn't do it for me like kohlrabi or potatoes do, but prepared this way, it's a different story.

MAKES 4 SERVINGS

1 Steam the broccoli for 3 minutes. It should be firm. Let it cool for 5 minutes then chop it.

2 Whisk the dressing ingredients in a large bowl.

3 Add the broccoli and onion, and toss well with your hands. Massage the broccoli gently with the dressing.

NORTH-AFRICAN CARROT SALAD

10 medium carrots, peeled

¼ cup parsley, chopped finely

2 tablespoons lemon juice

1 tablespoon harissa or 1 table paprika oil

3 garlic cloves, crushed

½ teaspoon ground cumin

Salt

My eldest dislikes all cooked carrot dishes except for this one. Though to be fair, the carrots in this salad are slightly steamed, therefore still firm. You're probably curious how I got him to try it in the first place. I simply bribed him. I offered him five bucks, which I ended up not paying him because he finished all of it and didn't leave any for us.

NOTE:

❖ If you don't have harissa, you can make paprika oil instead:
Put 1 tablespoon sweet paprika, 1 teaspoon hot paprika and ½ cup olive oil in a jar with a tight-fitting lid and shake vigorously. Let the paprika oil sit for about 30 minutes, to allow the paprika to settle at the bottom. Put only a spoonful of the oil in the salad (keep the rest in the fridge, to use again).

MAKES 4 SERVINGS

1 Cut the carrots in half and steam them for 4 minutes. Pierce them gently with a sharp knife. You should feel a little resistant. If the resistance is too strong, steam for 2 more minutes. Remove from the heat and wash with cold water. Slice the carrots and put in a medium bowl.

2 Slice the carrots and put in a medium bowl. Add next 5 ingredients and toss well.

3 Serve or store in a container in the fridge for up to 5 days.

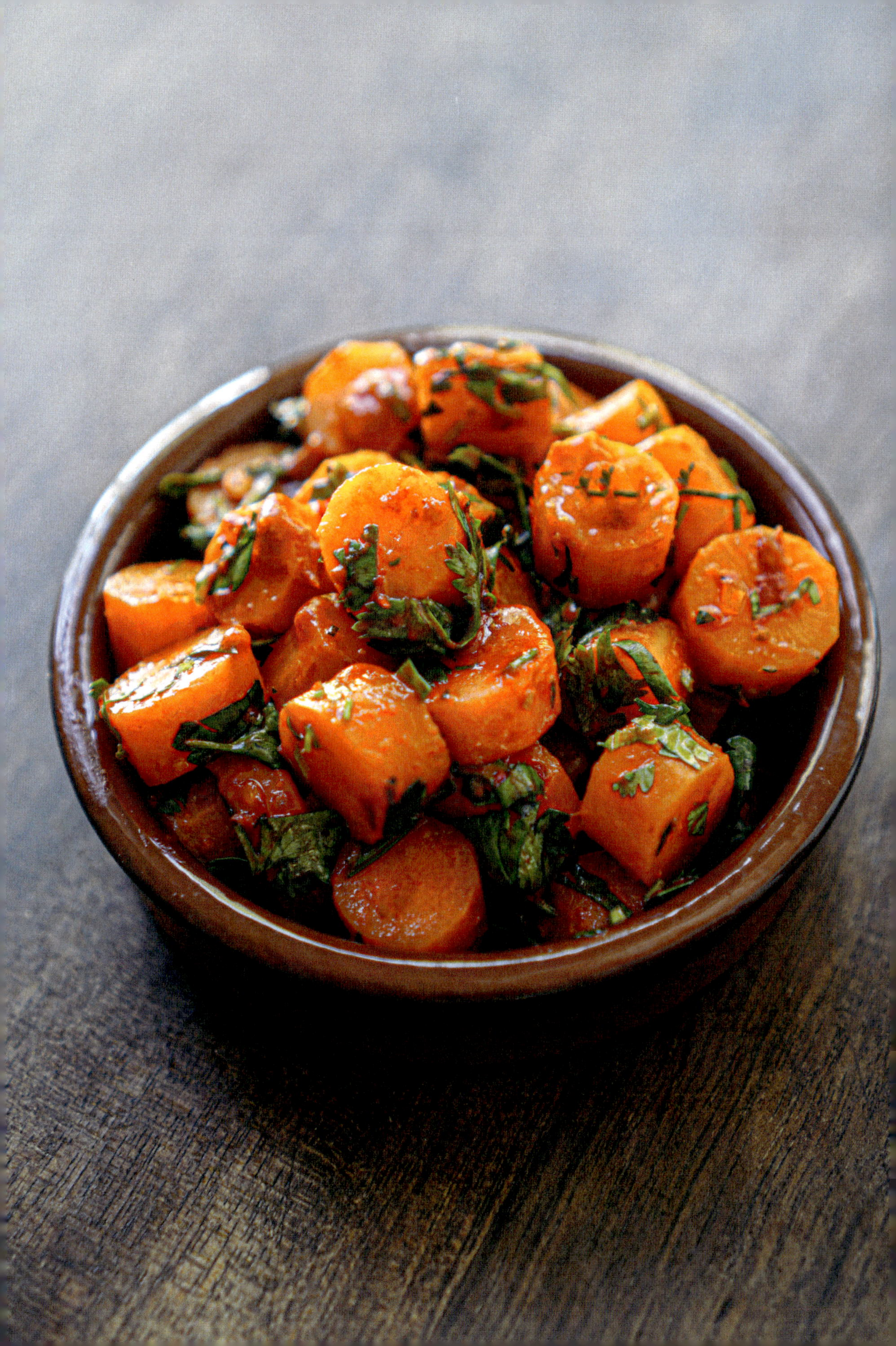

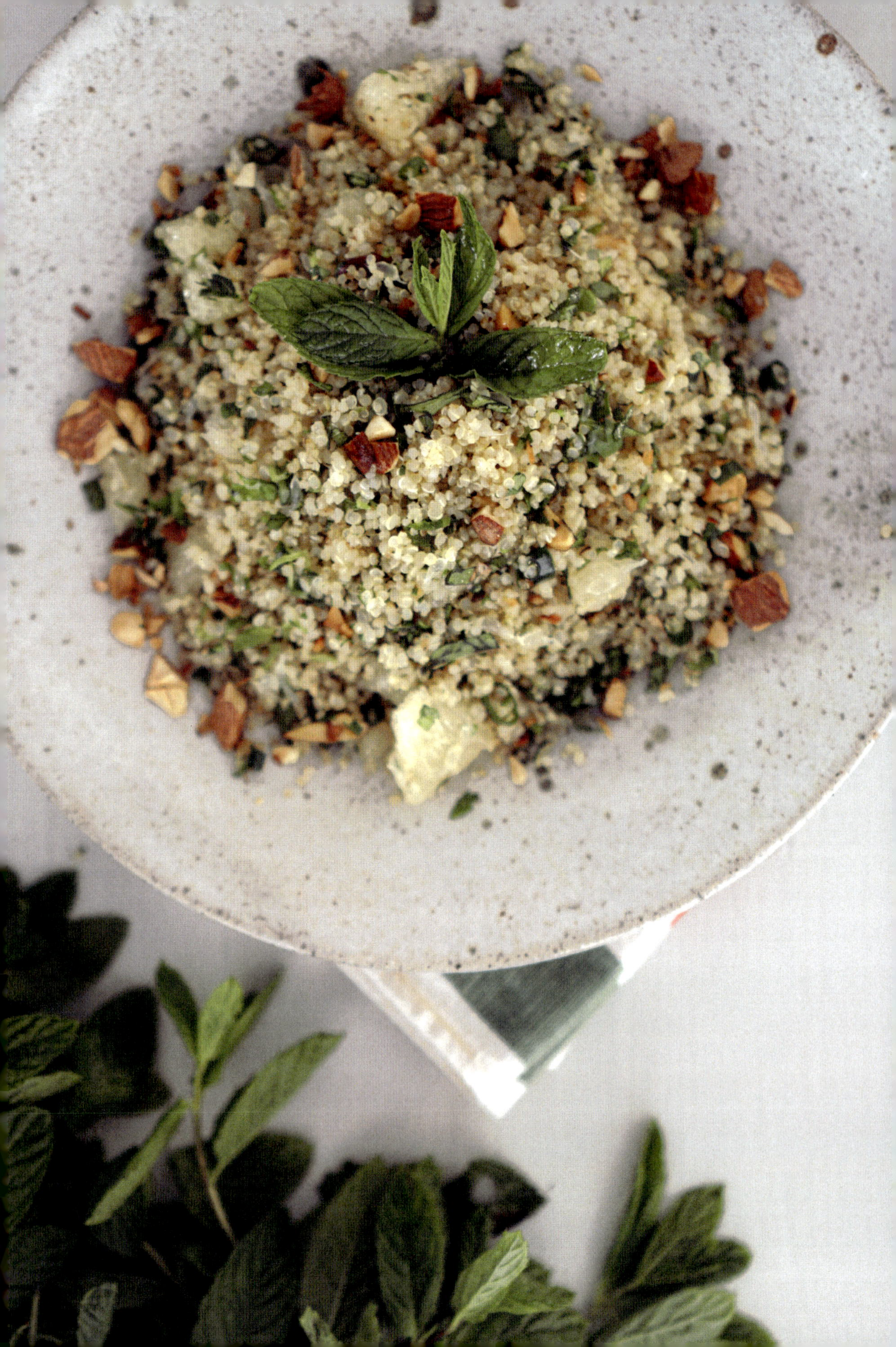

QUINOA, POMELO HERBS & TOASTED ALMONDS

4 cups cooked quinoa

2 cups pomelo segments

Small bunch of cilantro, chopped finely

Small bunch of parsley, chopped finely

2-3 scallions, chopped finely

10 mint leaves, chopped (optional)

Handful toasted almonds, chopped

¼ cup olive oil

2 tablespoons lemon juice

1 teaspoon apple cider vinegar (optional)

Salt

Black pepper

Pinch of cumin

For those of you who are not familiar with pomelo, it is the triple-H cup of citrus fruits. It has a thick green or yellow skin and massive red or yellow segments. The segments are pretty firm but juicy and sweet, without the acidity you get with oranges and grapefruit.

NOTES:

❖ You can make the salad with orange instead of pomelo.

❖ Brown rice, couscous or another grain instead of quinoa.

❖ Make it with any toasted nuts you like.

TO MAKE QUINOA:

1. Soak 1 cup quinoa in cold water for 5 minutes. Drain in a fine-mesh strainer and give it a 30 second rinse before putting it in a pot.

2. Put the quinoa in a pot with 2 cups of water. Bring to a boil over medium-high heat. Once boiling, reduce heat to lowest and cover the pot.

3. Simmer for about 15 minutes, or until the water is absorbed and the quinoa is tender. Remove from heat and let it sit, covered, for 5 minutes. Fluff with a fork before serving.

MAKES 4 SERVINGS

If the quinoa is warm, let it cool down before putting it in a medium bowl with the rest of the salad ingredients. Toss to combine. Taste and adjust seasoning, then serve.

Salad Ballads

ELVIS PARSLEY POTATO SALAD

20 medium waxy potatoes, about 4 pounds, rinsed and scrubbed thoroughly

¼ cup olive oil

1 teaspoon salt

1 teaspoon black pepper

A generous handful parsley or dill, chopped

1 garlic clove, crushed (optional)

1 heaping tablespoon mayonnaise or veganaise

If I had to choose just one potato salad to live on for the rest of my life, it would be this rockstar of potato salads.

MAKES 4 SERVINGS

1. Put the potatoes in a large pan, cover with water and boil until tender, about 20 minutes.

2. Drain the potatoes and transfer to a baking pan. Pour the olive oil over, season with the salt and pepper and toss well. Broil until they get a nice brown color.

3. Put the parsley, garlic and mayonnaise in a salad bowl and mix to combine.

4. Add the potatoes and toss well. Taste and add salt and pepper if necessary.

Salad Ballads

CELERY SALAD OVER CELERIAC HUMMUS

FOR THE HUMMUS

2 cups dried lima beans, soaked overnight

About 1 cup peeled diced celeriac (celery root)

¼ cup tahini

¼ cup or more fresh lemon juice

1-2 ice cubes

Salt

Pepper

FOR THE SALAD

2 stalks celery, peeled and finely diced

¼ cup finely chopped celery leaves

1 long red pepper or bell pepper, finely diced

1 tablespoon or more olive oil

1 tablespoon or more fresh lemon juice

½ teaspoon or more za'atar

Salt

Pepper

I didn't try to make a stunning-looking dish or impress friends who stopped by spontaneously. The only reason I garnished the hummus with the salad was that I didn't have enough salad for six people.

The advantage of serving a salad over hummus is that you don't need bread with it, assuming you're trying to cut back on carbs. This construction should work with any hummus, homemade or store-bought.

You'll see, the more you cook, the more experienced you'll get. And the more experience, the more creative you'll be.

Love is in the air everywhere I look around… Sing with me, or play it while preparing this dish.

A FEW THINGS BEFORE YOU START:

❖ You'll need a food processor for the lima celeriac hummus.

❖ If you want that ultra-smooth texture, remove the skins from the lima beans after you soaked them. It's worth the effort.

❖ You can make the celery salad a few hours ahead and keep it in the fridge until you're ready to serve.

❖ You can also eat this salad is over a peanut butter toast. Just trust the universe!

MAKES 2 TO 4 SERVINGS

1 To make the hummus: Drain and rinse the lima beans and put them in a medium saucepan. Cover with water and bring to a boil. Lower the heat and simmer for about 20 minutes, or until the beans are starting to get tender. Add the celeriac and continue to cook until the beans and celeriac are tender. Drain and let them cool down.

2 Put the celeriac and beans in the food processor with the tahini, ¼ cup lemon juice, salt, pepper and one ice cube, and process until smooth. Scrape down the sides. If the hummus is too thick, add another ice cube and process until creamy and soft. Taste and add more lemon juice, salt and pepper if necessary.

3 To make the salad: Combine celery, celery leaves, red pepper, 1 tablespoon olive oil, 1 tablespoon lemon juice and ½ teaspoon za'atar in a medium bowl. Season with salt and pepper, and toss well.

4 To serve: Spread the hummus on a large plate or serving bowl and put the salad in the center, over the hummus. Garnish with a light drizzle of olive oil and za'atar (optional).

COOKED SALADS

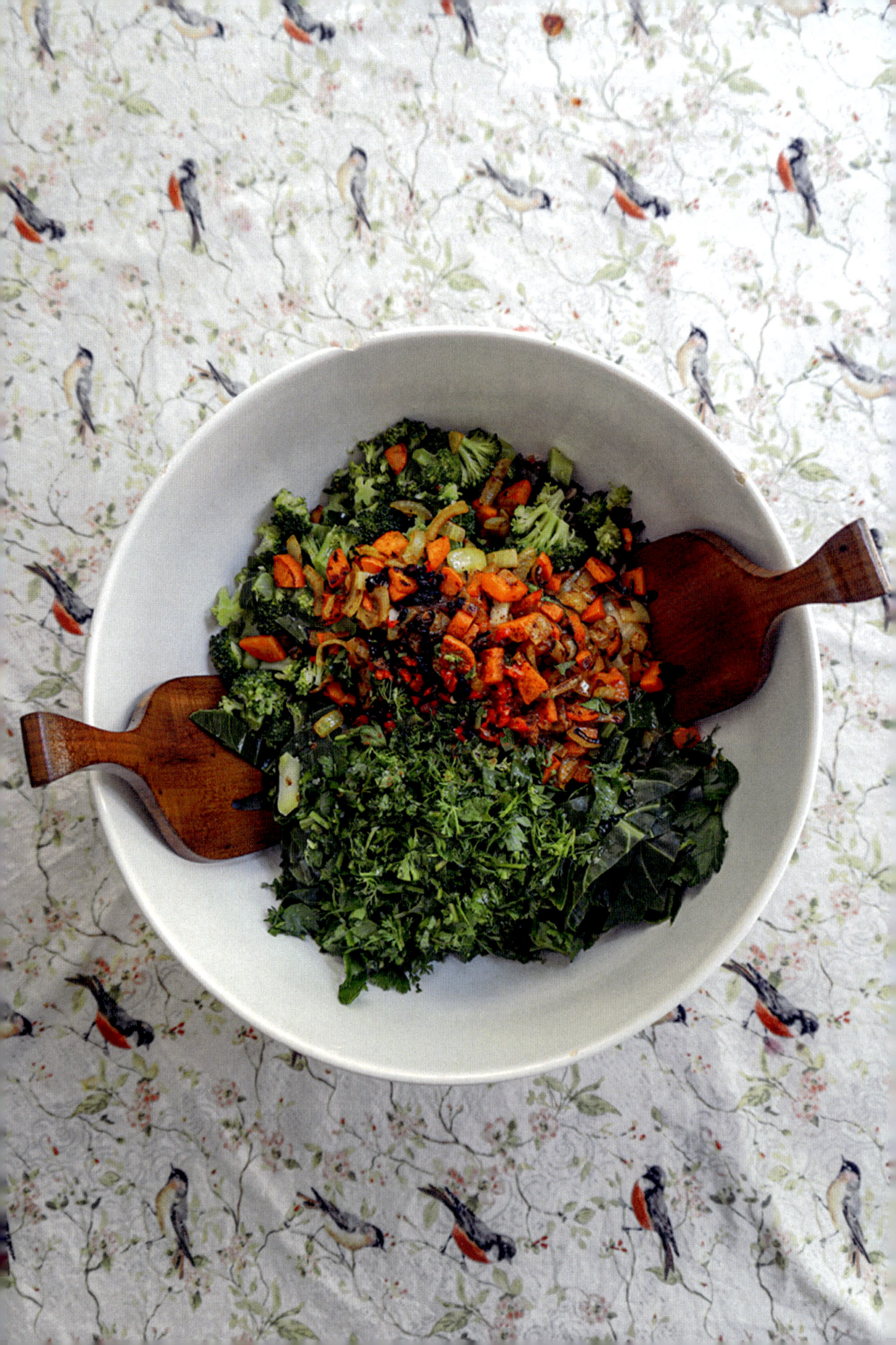

WILD THING, YOU MAKE MY RICE SING!

SALAD

3 tablespoons avocado oil

1 small onion, diced

1 medium sweet potato, diced

2 tablespoons barberries or raisins (optional)

1 head broccoli, separated into small florets

1 small bunch collard greens, Swiss chard or kale, chopped

2 cups cooked wild or brown rice

1 red chili, seeds removed and chopped finely (optional)

Handful cilantro or parsley or both, chopped finely

Salt

DRESSING

2 tablespoons olive oil

2 tablespoons tahini

1 tablespoon balsamic vinegar

1/4 teaspoon ground cinnamon

Salt

Optional Additions:

Avocado

Harissa

First thing first; wild rice and black rice are not the same thing. Wild rice is long and slender, with colors ranging from brown to black. It's got a chewy texture and a nutty flavor that's hard to beat. Black rice, on the other hand, is a deep black or purplish-black when raw. Once it's cooked, it turns a stunning dark purple. Compared to wild rice, it's shorter and rounder.

Wild rice has this wild and earthy flavor that begs to be paired with something soft and sweet like sweet potato. The two are like a match made in heaven. You can also make this with leftover brown rice.

Barberries (also known as zereshk) are the small, tart, red berries of the barberry shrub (Brberis vulgaris). They are commonly used in Iranian and Middle Eastern cuisine to add a pop of color and a sour, mild sweet flavor to dishes like rice pilafs, stews, and chicken dishes (Thank you, Wikipedia.)

MAKES 4 SERVINGS

1 make the salad: Put the avocado oil in a large skillet over medium-high heat. Add the onion, sweet potato and barberries and sauté on medium heat for 5 minutes, stirring occasionally.

2 Add ¼ cup water and salt and simmer for 10 minutes.

3 Add the broccoli and collard greens, and cook for 5 minutes. Transfer to a large bowl.

4 Add the cooked rice to the skillet and warm through, and add it to the vegetable bowl.

5 Add in chili, parsley and cilantro, and toss well. Serve with slices of avocado and harissa or hot sauce, if desired.

Salad Ballads

Beyond ORGANIC
SPRAY FREE
CABBAGE
$3.00 each

Salad Ballads

SMOKY CAFILOWER SALAD WITH TAHINI

FOR THE PAPRIKA OIL

¼ cup olive oil

1 teaspoon paprika

½ teaspoon smoked paprika

½ teaspoon salt

FOR THE SALAD

1 small cauliflower head, cut into florets

15 grape tomatoes, sliced in half

½ cup chopped cilantro

2 tablespoons tahini

2 tablespoons fresh lemon juice or apple cider vinegar.

This is a great salad to experiment with because cauliflower is like a second child; it can adapt to any flavor. After you make it my way, take the Indian highway and add Madras curry powder instead of the paprikas and skip the tahini. Or put a Taiwanese spin on it by replacing the olive oil with crunchy chili oil, using rice vinegar instead of lemon juice, and adding scallions. Bon voyage!

MAKES 2 TO 4 SERVINGS

1 Preheat the oven to 400°F (200°C).

2 Combine the paprika oil ingredients in a large high-rimmed baking tray. Add the cauliflower and toss to coat it evenly with the seasoned oil. Roast for 15 minutes, or until the cauliflower develops some color but remains slightly firm. Once done, let it cool slightly before adding to the salad.

3 Put the tomatoes and parsley in a large bowl.

4 Add the roasted cauliflower, tahini and lemon juice and toss well. You can keep the salad in the fridge for up to 1 day.

COOKED SALADS

AWFULLY GOOD CHICKPEA SALAD

2 tablespoons avocado oil or olive oil

1 small onion, roughly diced

1 hot green chili pepper or jalapeño, sliced

¼ teaspoon ground cumin

2 cups cooked or canned chickpeas, drained and rinsed

**2 medium tomatoes, peeled and diced
Handful parsley, chopped finely**

1 heaping tablespoon roasted pepper paste* or tomato paste

1 tablespoon or more lemon juice

½ teaspoon sumac (optional)

Salt

When mixing sweet vegetables such as onions and bell peppers with acidic tomatoes and lemon juice, a good thing happens. When adding tender chickpeas and sour sumac to that formula, that good thing becomes a great thing. Wait, it doesn't end here. When that mix of flavors and textures sits in the fridge for a day, this great thing becomes an awfully good chickpea salad. A Turkish-style salad.

NOTE:

❖ You can use store-bought pepper paste or make it yourself: Roast 1 red bell pepper or a bunch of sweet multicolored small peppers in the oven at 400°F (200°C) for 20 minutes or until tender. Peel off the skin, cut off the stems, remove the seeds and discard. Put them in a food processor with a short drizzle of olive oil, about 2 tablespoons, and process into a coarse paste. Store in a sterilized jar with a tight-fitting lid. The easiest way to sterilize a jar is to pour boiling water in it and let it sit for 3 minutes.

MAKES 2 TO 4 SERVINGS

1. Warm the oil in a small skillet on medium heat. Put in the cumin, onion, green chili pepper and salt, and sauté for 5 minutes, stirring occasionally.

2. Put the chickpeas in a medium salad bowl. Add in the sautéed onion, tomatoes, parsley, pepper paste, 1 tablespoon lemon juice and sumac and toss gently.

3. Taste and if necessary, add more lemon juice. Season with salt.

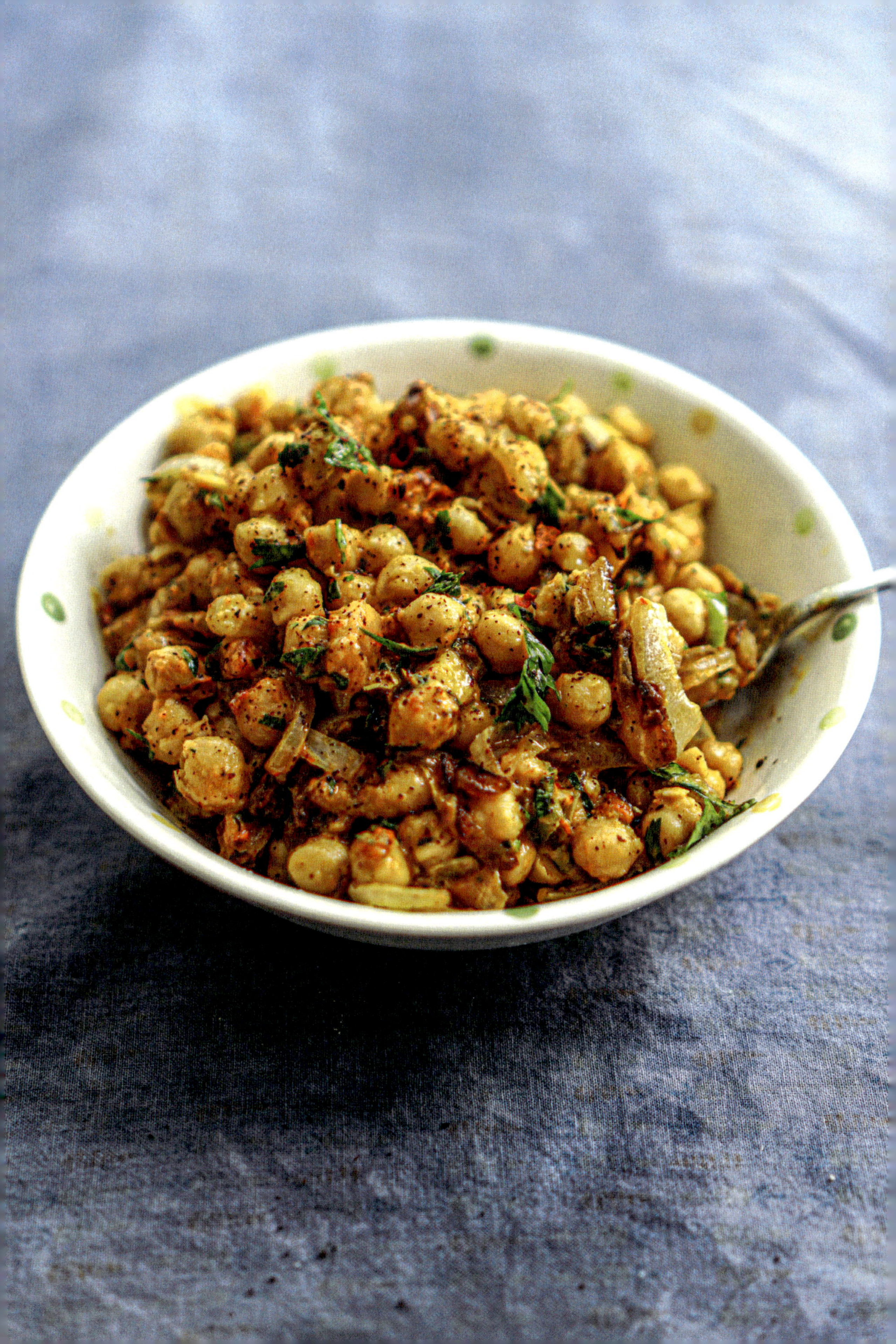

ABOUT THE AUTHOR

Shelly is a recipe developer, content creator, illustrator and the food blogger behind ShellysHumbleKitchen.com. Shelly was born and raised in Israel, where vegetables are as sacred as bread, by Jewish Moroccan parents who wouldn't sit down to eat unless there were at least three different types of salads on the table. She currently lives in Los Angeles with her husband and two children.

Wisdom-teeth-extraction-salad

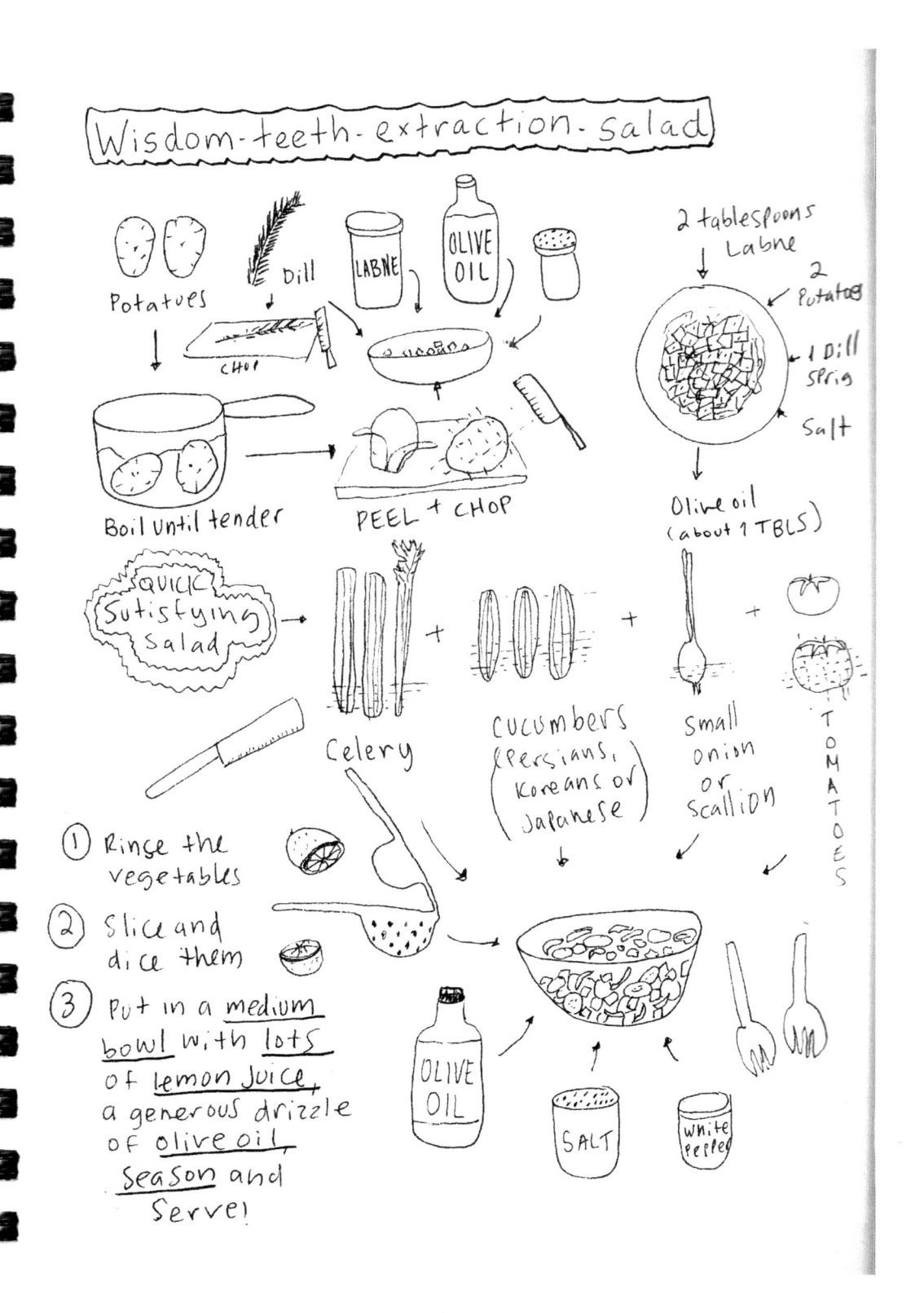

Potatoes · Dill · LABNE · OLIVE OIL

CHOP

Boil until tender → PEEL + CHOP

2 tablespoons Labne
2 Potatoes
1 Dill sprig
Salt
↓
Olive oil (about 1 TBLS)

QUICK Satisfying Salad

Celery + Cucumbers (Persians, Koreans or Japanese) + Small onion or scallion + TOMATOES

1. Rinse the vegetables
2. Slice and dice them
3. Put in a medium bowl with lots of lemon juice, a generous drizzle of olive oil, season and serve!

OLIVE OIL · SALT · white pepper

Salad Ballads

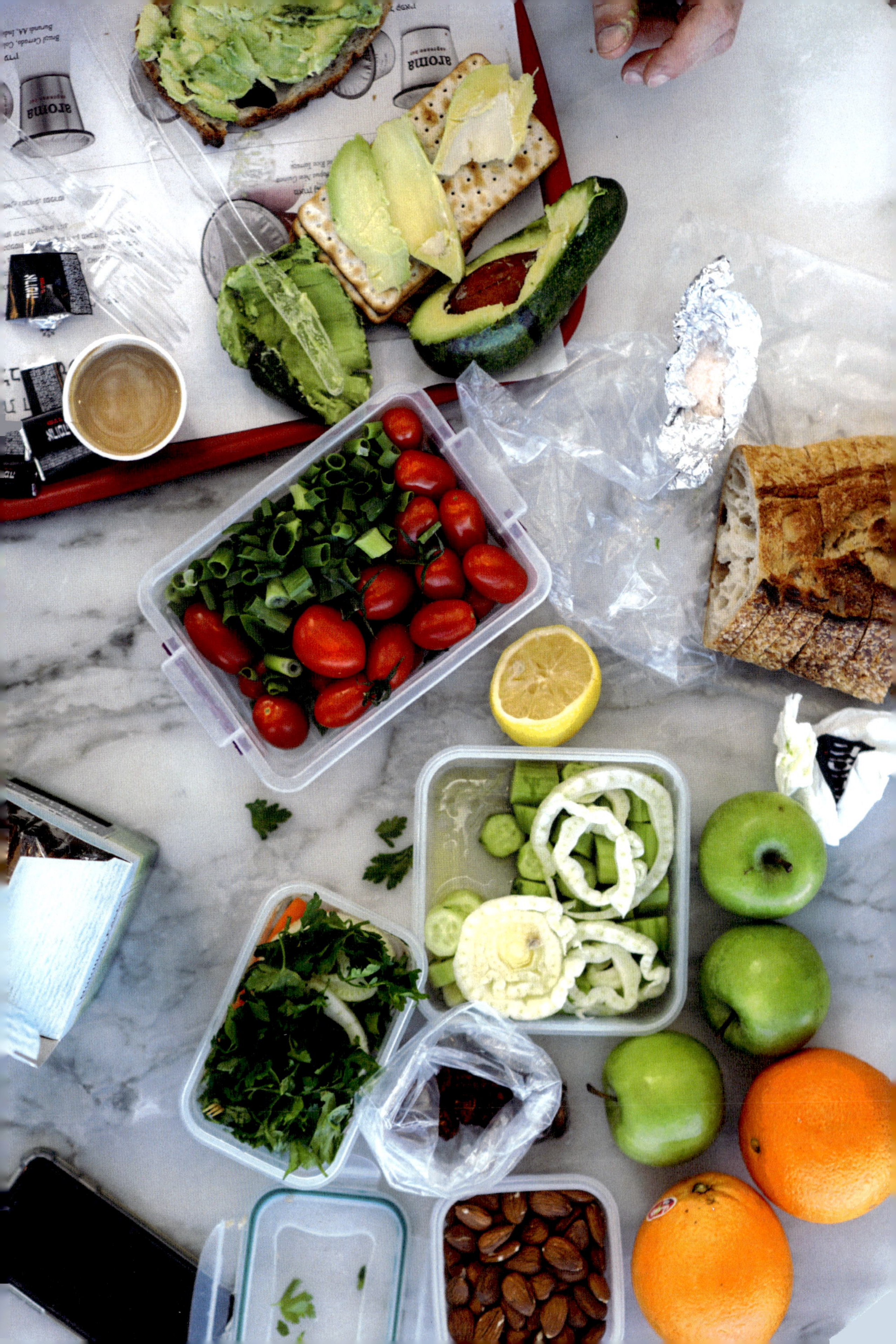
aroma

Salad Ballads

Made in the USA
Las Vegas, NV
08 April 2025

13f46a9f-51e3-4371-a6ad-f0061f1df8c2R01